An Age of Ambition

ENGLISH SOCIETY IN THE LATE MIDDLE AGES

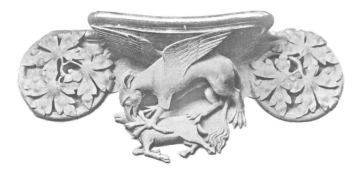

An Age of Ambition

ENGLISH SOCIETY IN THE LATE MIDDLE AGES

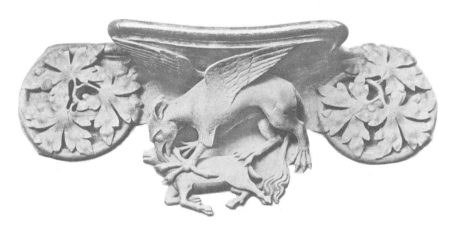

F. R. H. Du Boulay

Professor of Medieval History in the University of London

A Studio Book

THE VIKING PRESS

New York

Published in 1970 by The Viking Press, Inc.
625 Madison Avenue, New York, N.Y. 10022

Library of Congress catalog card number: 77-91318

Photoset in Malta by St Paul's Press Ltd
Printed in Great Britain by The Curwen Press, London, E.13

Contents

Illustrations

Black and white illustrations

P. 13: Burial of plague victims (Royal Library, Brussels, MS. 13076–7, fo. 24v); p. 16: King Henry VII (Victoria and Albert Museum, London. Crown copyright); p. 26: A travelling coach (Brit. Mus. Add. MS. 42,130 (Luttrell Psalter), fos. 181v, 182); p. 28: Pilgrims leaving Canterbury (Brit. Mus. Royal MS. 18 D ii, fo. 148); A bookshop (Brit. Mus. Cott. MS. Tiberius A vii, fo. 91v); p. 29: A section of the 'Gough map' (Bodleian Library, Oxford); p. 33: A physician treats a patient (Brit. Mus. Royal MS. 20 C vii, fo. 78v); p. 39: Leprous beggar-woman (Brit. Mus. Lansdowne MS. 451, fo. 127); Rich and poor (Walters Art Gallery, Baltimore, MS. W. 174, fo. 125); p. 42: A fifteenth-century impression of London (Brit. Mus. Royal MS. 16 F ii, fo. 73); p. 43:

Carpenter and mason (Brit. Mus. Royal MS. 15 E ii, fo. 265); Building works (Brit. Mus. Cott. MS. Nero E ii, fo. 73); p. 44: A master mason consults the King (Brit. Mus. Cott. MS. Nero D i, fo. 23v); p. 46: Water mill (Brit. Mus. Royal MS. 15 E vi, fo. 4v); p. 47: Sheep shearing (Brit. Mus. Add. MS. 17,012, fo. 6); Dyeing (Brit. Mus. Royal MS. 15 E iii, fo. 269); Weaving on a handloom (Brit. Mus. Royal MS. 17 E iv, fo. 87v); The Master of the Wool Staple (Brit. Mus. Royal MS. 14 E iv, fo. 169v); p. 48: Flemish ships (Brit. Mus. Harl. MS. 4425, fo. 86); Iron miner of the Forest of Dean (All Saints Church, Newland, Gloucs.; National Monuments Record); p. 49: Blacksmith (Brit. Mus., woodcut from William Caxton's *Game and Play of the Chess*, ? 1483); p. 50: Ploughing (Brit. Mus. Cott. MS. Augustus v, fo. 161v); p. 51: A barn (Brit. Mus. Royal MS. E vi, fo. 62); p. 52: House of the wool merchant, William Grevel (National Monuments Record); p. 53: Cloth merchant's house at Coggeshall, Essex (National Monuments Record); p. 64: The Court of Chancery (Library of the Inner Temple, London; Misc. MS. 188); p. 69: A gentleman dresses in comfort by the fire (Brit. Mus. Royal MS. 2 B vii, fo. 72v); p. 78: A Kentish peasant (Library of Lambeth Palace; Register of William Courtenay, fo. 337v); Friars depicted with a devil on their backs (Corpus Christi College, Cambridge, MS. 180, fo. 1); p. 79: A friar hears a confession (Bodleian Library, Oxford; MS. Douce 131, fo. 126); p. 82: A 'scolding wife' (Henry VII's chapel, Westminster Abbey; National Monuments Record); p. 85: A diagram of consanguinity (Brit. Mus. Royal MS. 6 E vi, fo. 196); The wedding ring (Brit. Mus. Royal MS. 6 E vi, fo. 104); p. 87: Lovers' meeting (Brit. Mus. Harl. MS. 4431, fo. 376); Portrait by Holbein said to be of John Colet (Brit. Mus., Dept. of Prints and Drawings); p. 99: A wedding (Pierpont Morgan Library, New York; MS. M 394, fo. 9v); The wedding of Henry V and Catherine of France (Brit. Mus. Royal MS. 20 E vi, fo. 9v); p. 105: Adultery (Brit. Mus. Royal MS. 6 E vi, fo. 61); p. 111: Carving at high table (Brit. Mus. Add. MS. 12,228, fo. 126); p. 114: An English bedroom (Brit. Mus. Cott. MS. Julius E iv, art. 6, fo. 1); p. 117: Schoolboy being beaten (Brit. Mus. Burney MS. 275, fo. 94); A school scene (Brit. Mus. Royal MS. 17 E iii, fo. 93v); p. 124: A knight being armed for combat (Pierpont Morgan Library, New York; MS. M 775, fo. 122v); p. 130 Coronation of a king (Library of Westminster Abbey, London; *Liber Regalis*, fo. 1v); p. 132: A messenger to the king (Brit. Mus. Sloane MS. 2433 (1), fo. 63v); p. 133: Richard Beauchamp, Earl of Warwick (Brit. Mus. Cott. MS. Julius E iv, art. 6, fo. 25); p. 136: 'Traylebaston': English thugs with offensive weapons (Brit. Mus. Cott. MS. Nero D ii, fo. 195); Parliament at Westminster (Brit. Mus. Harl. MS. 1319, fo. 57); p. 145: St Michael weighing the souls of the dead (Victoria and Albert Museum, London. Crown copyright); Pope,

Emperor, and King, with crowned skeletons (Brit. Mus. Harl. MS. 2917, fo. 119); p. 150: The deathbed of Richard Whittington (The Mercers' Company, London; MS. 'Ordinances of Whittington's Hospital); Our Lady of Pity (Brit. Mus. Add. MS. 29,433, fo. 174); The deposition from the Cross (Victoria and Albert Museum, London. Crown copyright); Death Riding; drawing by Dürer (Brit. Mus., Dept. of Prints and Drawings); p. 153: Mass for the dead (Pierpont Morgan Library, New York; MS. M 359, fo. 119v); p. 155; The chantry chapel of Bishop Waynflete (Winchester Cathedral; National Monuments Record); p. 157: An English pilgrim (E. Tristram, *English Wall Painting of the Fourteenth Century*, Routledge, London, 1955, Plate 25); p. 161: François Villon (*Le grand testament villon*, 1489); Warden and scholars of New College, Oxford (New College, Oxford; MS. 288 (Chandler MS.), fo. 3v); p. 167: St Thomas Aquinas (Florence, Museo di S. Marco; Mansell Collection); p. 168: William of Ockham (Gonville and Caius College, Cambridge, MS. 464/571); p. 173: Nicholas of Cusa (Church of S. Pietro in Vincoli, Rome; Mansell Collection).

The device reproduced on the title page is from a photograph of a misericord in Wells cathedral, depicting a griffin. It is reproduced by courtesy of the National Monuments Record.

Abbreviations

References to sources in the footnotes of this book are mostly given in full for the convenience of readers, but there are a few instances where space may be better saved by describing the source once for all. These are given below.

Cely Papers:

The Cely Papers: selections from the correspondence and memoranda of the Cely family, merchants of the Staple, 1475–1488, edited by H. E. Malden, Camden Third Series, volume I, 1900.

Paston Letters:

The Paston Letters, 1422–1509 (a reprint of the edition of 1872–5, with a Supplement and Introduction by James Gairdner), 4 volumes, 1900–8.

Plumpton Correspondence:	*The Plumpton Correspondence*, edited by T. Stapleton, Camden Old Series, volume IV, 1839.
Stonor Letters:	*The Stonor Letters and Papers*, edited by C. L. Kingsford, Camden Third Series, volumes XXIX and XXX, 1919.
Statutes of the Realm:	*Statutes of the Realm*, Record Commission, London, 1810–28.

Acknowledgements

In preparing this book and its illustrations I have received generous help from many quarters. I acknowledge with gratitude the trouble taken by my colleagues, Mrs Caroline Barron and Dr Geoffrey Britten, by Miss Sarah Jeacock, and by Mr Peter Ford and Mr Anthony Raven of Thomas Nelson & Sons Ltd.

Permission to quote from *The Book of Beasts* was kindly given by the Trustees for the copyrights of the late T. H. White, from the work of T. S. Eliot by Faber & Faber Ltd and by Harcourt, Brace & World Inc., and from his own translation of Villon by Mr Galway Kinnell.

For the reproduction of pictures in their possession or custody permission was kindly granted by the Royal Library, Brussels, the Victoria and Albert Museum, London, the Trustees of the British Museum, the Bodleian Library, Oxford, the Walters Art Gallery, Baltimore, the National Monuments Record, the Master of the Bench of the Inner Temple, London, the Archbishop of Canterbury and the Trustees of Lambeth Palace Library, the Master and Fellows of Corpus Christi College, Cambridge, the Pierpont Morgan Library, New York, the Dean and Chapter of Westminster, the Mercers' Company, London, Routledge & Kegan Paul Ltd, the Warden and Fellows of New College, Oxford, and the Master and Fellows of Gonville and Caius College, Cambridge.

F. R. H. DU BOULAY

July 1969

Charme profonde, magique, dont nous grise
Dans le présent le passé restauré!
Ainsi l'amant sur un corps adoré
Du souvenir cueille la fleur exquise.
— CHARLES BAUDELAIRE, *Spleen et Idéal*, XI

1 The Myth of Decline

In the world of medieval studies historians of the late Middle Ages still have to work a little more persuasively than others to justify themselves. This was clearer in the Oxford of the late 1940s than it is today. Great teachers make great traditions, and such traditions become too dignified for early death. Perhaps they were quicker in France to see that the suffering of the fourteenth and fifteenth centuries was fertile. While English undergraduates were usually directed to Stubbs's *Select Charters*, which stopped in 1307, French scholars were already repairing the mental desolation of their country by returning to an earlier desolation and finding in the century of Joan of Arc new life under the apparent ruins. But in England the earlier past still reigned securely. The ghost of Bishop Stubbs was repeating that England had passed in the fourteenth century from an age of heroism to one of chivalry, to heartless selfishness and moral degradation. The first of the great *Oxford Histories of England* to be written in the medieval field stayed within the apostolic tradition. Its disciples taught in our schools, and whoever has marked school examination papers will understand the weary time-lag between research and reception, and the way in which the history of scholars becomes the folklore of the General Certificate of Education. Ideas which were good for their time are simplified into the words of a story that children, being children, commit to heart and repeat: waning, sterility, abuse, corruption and decline. More precisely, the fifteenth century is still supposed above all to suffer from crippling demerits which may be classified into four. Under the influence of Shakespeare's history plays and the premature interpretation of the Paston Letters, it was seen as an age of exceptional violence and lawlessness. Secondly, it was an age of cultural barrenness between the time of Chaucer and Langland at one end and the Tudor poets and humanists at the other. Huizinga had done his best for France and Burgundy, but this was not England; his very title, *The Waning of the Middle Ages*, had set an oppressive and negative tone, and the book's excessive literariness had circumvented too many historical actualities. Thirdly, there was the more sophisticated argument that the period from about 1350 to 1470 was one of general economic recession in which declining national income was proved by almost every available statistical index, whether in agricultural production or in industry and trade. The conclusions drawn were that the landlords suffered and, if some sections of the population grew comparatively richer, technical innovation marked time, investment lagged, national poverty prevailed. The fourth demerit was the most familiar of all. It was an age of moral and religious decline, ruled by lechery (especially of the clergy), by avarice, superstition, witchcraft and the fear of death. The church was enslaved by its institutional rules. Men were 'earthy, selfish and grasping'.

Of course, there are truths in all these simplifications. But they suffer from the overstatement of repetition; they leave out of account the positive aspects of the age and, worst of all, they do not explain in any satisfactory form why things were as they were.

If a change of emphasis is needed (the aim of this essay), it is not undertaken in the spirit of counter-morality or to replace an orthodoxy by one more lasting. The wish is to explain a selection of past problems with the sympathy due from a present time that is beset by its own, not altogether dissimilar ones, and not to ridicule great historians of an older generation. Historians are no more detached from their own times than philosophers, and it should not be shocking if in studying the past they feel a special concern with whatever seems to foreshadow the interests of their own day.

The great constitutional and legal tradition which for so long dominated historical studies in England, for example, can clearly not be explained entirely apart from the rightful admiration men of letters felt for the expertise of their own nineteenth-century English government. Similarly, the ecclesiastical preoccupations of the nineteenth century — that most religious age — brought with them a fresh interest in medieval religious organization and thought. In such ways history continues, like philosophy, to function as a language of explanation, offering to every generation a new chance to identify and thus to comfort itself by new arrangements of evidence.

There is, in fact, a fresh modern interest which gathers strength from year to year and in which historians find themselves involved, namely in the structure of society. It would now be short-sighted of a historian to shirk at least a passing familiarity with new disciplines — anthropology and psychology as well as economics. Old-timers tend to scoff, thinking perhaps of tedious descriptions of 'everyday life', or withdrawing from the unclean touch of sociologists whom they suspect, not altogether without reason, of being uninterested in people. But it is hard to live through a society's transformation and to remain unmoved and, being moved, equally hard not to look back and reflect how it is that at certain periods the life of a family, a class or a nation can so radically alter in its hopes, achievements and habits. This is the justification for the present book.

The time-span it covers requires a closer look. The 'later Middle Ages' was a period of particular development, not just an ossification of what had gone before, still less a mere sequence of regnal years. We may take it to begin in the second half of the fourteenth century, a period which contains a series of astonishing landmarks.

First in historical order came the Black Death, which swept into England in the autumn of 1348 and killed, within a year, a fraction of the population which no one can determine with certainty, but which was probably not less than a third. The great war with France had not long been renewed, and the attractions of military service, which offered rewards in money and changed horizons to the able-bodied, removed from their labours in England even more men who were needed in productive work. Medieval men had few of today's easy answers about supply and demand, but, whether explained as God's judgement on wickedness or greed, the economic laws operated just the same. A consequence both immediate and long-lasting was the demand for

Burial of plague victims at Tournai, 1352. The age began with epidemic.

higher wages and an impatience with old customs. In 1349 and 1350 came the first attempts to freeze wages and direct labour. Men were to ask no more for a day's work than formerly, and employers, too, were penalized for making higher offers. The Ordinance of Labourers (1349), made by the King's Council, was given the authority of Parliament in the Statute of Labourers of 1350. About the same time the Archbishop of Canterbury issued a constitution known from its opening words as *Effrenata cupiditas* — 'unbridled cupidity' — which applied similar conditions to the numerous clergy who worked for stipends, rebuking them in moral terms, understood by all and credited by some, for their demands. Needless to say, solemn laws do not stem such rising tides. This was to be partly recognized by re-enactments like that of 1388 when Parliament at Cambridge made some concessions, realizing that employers no less than work-people had been hostile to the laws on wage-restraint. The problem was one which prevailed throughout the period covered by this book and gives the period a basic economic unity. But its beginnings were sufficiently sudden to form an intelligible starting-point.

Although the first plague allowed a fairly unspecialized agrarian society to carry on even after the massive loss of life, the reduction in human population meant that labour became markedly more expensive. For the same reason foodstuffs became relatively cheaper. Despite bad harvests from time to time, there were, none the less, fewer mouths to feed, and if the meek did not quickly inherit the earth, there was more land available per head of the population, better land to choose from, quicker chances of inheriting or acquiring and, for that matter, of running away to a better life beyond the manorial confines. As time went on, the difference in wages between the skilled and the unskilled began to close up — a classic sign of labour scarcity — and even in the fifteenth century, as the plague became more restricted to towns or limited areas and less lethal in its impact, a state of elevated wages in relation to the basic cost of living continued. If a graph of wheat prices is imposed upon a graph of real wages between 1300 and 1500, it will look roughly like a pair of scissors, the blade of wages ascending, the blade of food prices pointing downwards. What has been called the 'golden age of the wage labourer' is now explained by economic historians as the 'price-scissors', and it was the same in France (*'scission des prix'*) and in Germany (*'Preisscheren'*). The more detailed effects must be left to a later chapter, but the total result was that men whose parents and grandparents had been desperately poor now had a greater share of the country's wealth to spend on things other than food. Not surprisingly, men and women began to appear and behave differently. Finer clothes dignified people whom their social superiors in a stratified society thought of as mean and even bestial. New suppliers arrived to cater to new demands in clothing, headgear, footwear, household goods and personal possessions, and the suppliers themselves did well out of the situation. It was indeed a situation paralleled time and again in a world where catastrophe or invention redistributes wealth. Perhaps today there are a few reactionaries to frown at the Woolworth's revolution, just as there were gentry to look askance at munition workers in fur coats during the First World War, but in the late fourteenth century it could still be a matter for legislation. A series of 'sumptuary laws' attempted to classify the population by status, betraying in its very wording that status could be governed at least partly by income, and requiring that those of mean estate confine themselves to simple apparel. Agricultural labourers, for example, were told in 1363 that if they had less than 40s.' worth of property they might wear no cloth but blanket and russet wool at 1s. the cloth. Yet reiteration proves only such laws' ineffectiveness, whether in snubbing the upstart or protecting the home market against the import of expensive luxuries.

Concurrently, there came an upward movement of criticism and protest — by bondmen against bondage, menials against gentry, knightly persons against aristocrats, and almost everyone against an entrenched clergy who operated a religion that appeared formalistic and over-endowed. The criticism was expressed in literature as well as by violence. Not that the spirit was wholly new, but by the last quarter of the fourteenth century it had become overt and menacing, calling out counter-measures of bitterness and terror. The Great Revolt of 1381 was crushed with a satisfaction undisguised in the Chronicles. Lollards, who at first seemed lunatics, had by 1401 become subject to the penalty of death. Those parliamentary Knights who spoke against the government and its inept, dishonest and expensive handling of the war in 1376 were regarded by the King's uncle, John of Gaunt, England's most powerful noble, with bewildered anger.

These occurrences, simplified though they are for an introductory chapter, serve to characterize the beginning of our period.

It is more difficult to decide when the period ends. The year 1485 as a familiar dynastic landmark may be dismissed with little argument. It was not the end of the crisis in authority, and only by hindsight a political milestone, since no one could be sure at that moment that the Tudors would stay firmly on the throne. There is some reason to regard the 1470s and 1480s as a terminal period, for population and rents began to recover, especially in the south and east of England; Edward IV appeared to be producing a financial stability for the crown, and an economic upsurge began to be visible. Yet a chronological scheme that is allowed to end so near the margin of change is unsatisfying. There would be arguable sense in ending the 'Middle Ages' in the 1530s, at a moment when England was about to experience a rise of prices steep enough to dwarf all changes since the time of the Roman Empire. In the same decade, 1530—40, came administrative changes connected with the work of Thomas Cromwell, and a lonely Thomas More lost his head for the lost cause of papal jurisdiction. Even so, it is clear that stability had returned by the end of Henry VII's reign in 1509, and to embrace so much of Tudor history as medieval is unnecessary to the main purpose of this book. Since this book is written basically as an economic and social explanation, a distinguished economic historian may be allowed to have the last word. Professor Phelps-Brown sees Henry VIII's first year, 1510, as the moment when real wages began to fall for the first time in the whole medieval period.* As the 'price-scissors' then begin to close, men who had lived through a time of amelioration were entering a new age, when the population would rise once again, prices take a sharp turn upwards, self-expression become more vivacious, and successful men with short family histories would consolidate their gains at the expense of a crowd of newly poor.

King Henry VII: bust by Pietro Torregiano. Recovery and fresh changes.

*E. H. Phelps-Brown and Sheila Hopkins, 'Seven Centuries of the Prices of Consumables Compared with Builders' Wage-rates', in *Essays in Economic History*, edited by E. M. Carus-Wilson, II (1962), p. 189.

16

2 The Identity
of England

What was England to Englishmen in the fifteenth century? Three words await reflection: nation, nationality, nationalism. To medieval men it would appear natural enough to compare social or political development with the growing organism of the child and the man, and this tracing of a parallel between the life of a person and that of a body politic may be useful in trying to describe the national identity of late medieval England itself.

Very small children have the touching confidence of ignorance and distinguish between friend and foe only with untutored instinct. But as their home takes shape their confidence becomes enlarged to include neighbours, friends and countrymen. What is familiar may grow dearer by contrast with what is alien. Conversely, the outer world of aliens may appear soon and easily as hostile, sharpening the sense of what since birth has without self-consciousness been trusted and loved. How poignant seem even the casual good-nights of home in the memory of a boy during his first long night amidst strangers! The life of a people is not unlike this, though of greater complexity. Its simpler members are home-bound and speak of men from the next tribe or village or shire as foreigners long after their more adventurous kinsmen, educated or in search of improvement, have become grown members of the world. Nor do a society's horizons grow wider at a uniform pace or without regressions. Poverty and technical stagnation may retard the whole process. Money makes free and travel is a kind of freedom. Likewise, external enmities formed by the friction of travel may strengthen internal self-consciousness and impress compatriots with a more urgent need for one another. So a strange mixture of internal development and external opposition produces sentiments of identity which become habitual, forging nationhood through community of speech and interest and ultimately, perhaps, a striving for mastery over others that may be termed nationalism.

Nation as a word follows a development corresponding to these human attitudes. *Natio* was a rare but genuine classical Latin term. It began by denoting one's origin by birth and was more or less equivalent to *genus*, *stirps* and *familia*. Later it took on a more contemptuous connotation: 'tribe' or 'set'. For the Latins, nations were barbarians, not themselves. Cicero usually applied the word to distant and uncouth peoples – *'gentes nationes-que'* – and in ecclesiastical Latin, with Tertullian, it took on the meaning of heathen as opposed to Christians. Would not readers of the Psalms have this in mind as they asked, 'Why do the nations so furiously rage together?'

Much later, when Christendom had become richer and its members more mobile, in the twelfth and thirteenth centuries, the term *natio* found a fresh technical use in the young universities where men came from afar to study. The greater number of these students were grouped at Paris, Bologna and Oxford into 'nations' which had little to do with political origins, let alone nation-states. At Paris, for example, the youthful body of arts students were grouped into separate 'nations' of Picards, Normans and so forth. At Bologna a student's 'nation' might, if he came from Italy, at first derive from a single Italian town, though soon these tiny Italian nations coalesced into those of Tuscany, Lombardy and Rome. The 'nations' from north of the Alps were larger and, as we shall see, acquired a solidity based upon language and strengthened by the need for protection felt by colonies of strangers in a strange land. At Oxford the 'nations' of arts students never got beyond the distinction between North and South, a division which does not go unperceived at the present day.

The matter of language is fundamental to the growth of nationhood. True, the clerks spoke Latin, but outside the lecture hall Latinity waned. By the fifteenth century, too, the languages of western Europe were approaching the standard forms understood today within the political boundaries of England, France and Germany. The German 'nation' at Bologna University was organized under the rule of proctors who kept books of their acts, and in one of these may be found a statement of far-reaching interest:

> It is fitting for the members to be organized into one body, lest by their wandering dispersal the body becomes contemptible. . . . We therefore order that those studying in the renowned city who are from the nation of the Germans, that is, *all who have the native German tongue, even if their domicile is elsewhere* . . . shall be understood as the college of the German nation. But because Bohemians, Moravians, Lithuanians and Danes have from early times been accepted into our nation . . . we embrace them and join them to us. . . .*

*This statement was made in 1497 in the memorandum book kept by the German students in the University of Bologna, and can be found in *Acta Nationis Germanicae universitatis Bononiensis*, edited by Carlo Malagola, Berlin, 1887, p. 4.

Such reasoning calls to mind the issue of language, which is crucial. In fourteenth-century England, whatever else he spoke, every native spoke a form of English. French was being forgotten and it had to be specially taught at Oxford. In 1353 it was ordered that English be spoken in all cases in the London Sheriff's courts. In 1362 the same order was made for the high courts of law. In 1363 the Chancellor opened Parliament for the first time with a speech in English. In 1385 John of Trevisa said that 'nowadays boys know no more French than their left heel', and in 1404 two ambassadors to France admitted that 'we are as ignorant of French as of Hebrew'. Poets wrote for an English public. Yet it was still an English of diverse dialects, not perfectly understood in the same form throughout the country. A well-known passage from Trevisa, a schoolmaster who died in 1402, runs:

Also Englishmen had from the beginning three manners of speech, northern, southern and midland speech in the middle of the land, as they come from three manner of people of Germania. None the less, by mingling first with Danes and afterwards with Normans, in many the *contray longage is apayred and som useth straunge wlafferynge, chiterynge, harrynge, and garrynge grisbaytinge. . . .*

And he went on to say that Midlanders could understand both their northern and southern neighbours, while North and South could not understand each other. The Northumbrians were especially hard to make out, as their language *'is so scharp, slitting and frotynge and unschepe'*. Kings themselves rarely went far to the north for long. The Midlands speech was becoming the basis of modern English. Because the London dialect was that of the Court, the Government, and of the royal Justices on Assize, the East Midlands speech was becoming standard and so is the basis of Modern English. Chaucer's 'Reeve's Tale' contrasts northern and southern speech, because throughout the two clerks speak in broad northern:

> John highte that oon, and Aleyn highte that oother;
> Of o toun were they born, that hightè Strother,
> Fer in the North, I kan nat tellè where. . . . *

There will be more to say later about English speech in the context of class structure, but it is time to continue with the discussion of nationality.

The word 'nation', already long used in universities, was taken up at the time of the Conciliar movement in the early fifteenth century in a slightly different setting. Apart from church reform, the problem at the Council of Constance was, of course, to elect a single pope in place of the three claimants

---

*The Canterbury Tales: 'Reeve's Tale', lines 4013—15.

who were dividing the allegiance of Christendom. To this end the delegations from various countries, already conscious of their own hardening identities, were housed for months on end in different quarters of the German-speaking city. In place of the College of Cardinals, it was in fact national delegations that were manoeuvring and parleying with each other for a solution. The French were conscious of some superiority, proud of their university at Paris, and embittered by the recent result at the battle of Agincourt, but were prepared to admit the English as allies to offset the influence of Italian cardinals. As for the English, victorious and clamant, they chose to regard themselves as a nation equal to the French, and used these words:

... whether a nation be understood as a people marked off from others by blood relationship and habit of unity, or by peculiarities of language (the most sure and positive sign and essence of a nation in divine and human law) ... or whether nation be understood, as it should be, as a territory equal to that of the French nation, England is a real nation. ...

Their claim won the day. Yet it would be wholly wrong to imagine that the political nationhood of England had thus emerged in the minds of a handful of professors. The story must be taken further back to become intelligible.

It could just be imagined that the Norman invaders of 1066 would have been absorbed within two or three generations into an English-speaking society which thus would have possessed at least a linguistic basis of identity. But with the arrival of Henry of Anjou as Henry II in 1154 a new injection of French culture was received. A more vital stage in the sundering of England and France came when King John was driven from Normandy in 1204 and decisively lost his Angevin Empire by 1214. The aristocracy was then faced with the important decision whether to be English or French; and the breach was widening and becoming usual in the thirteenth century. A basis of political nationality was being laid even before the linguistic one of which some account has already been taken. In 1242, the chronicler Matthew Paris tells us that the king of the French issued a harsh order that English merchants trafficking in his kingdom should be seized. By doing so, Matthew continued, he inflicted a heavy wound on the ancient reputation of Gaul, which once offered asylum and protection to all refugees and even exiles if they were peaceable, and it was for this reason, he claimed, that it first obtained the name of France in the vulgar tongue. When this disgraceful wantonness came to the ears of the king of England he gave a like order that all French merchants who were in England should suffer a well-deserved retribution.

20

Two years later, in 1244, the chronicler shows the conflict being taken a stage further when

the king of the French assembled at Paris all dwellers beyond the sea who had estates in England and thus addressed them: — 'whatever inhabitant of my realm has estates in England, seeing that he cannot fitly serve two masters, must completely and irrevocably attach himself to the king of England.' For this reason, some who had estates in England abandoned them, and devoted themselves to their French properties, and others did the reverse. And when the king of England was informed of this, he directed that all the natives of the realm of France, and especially the Normans [those who had recently come from Normandy], should be ousted from the lands they held in England.

In this way, the beginnings of an identifiable English nationality may be seen from a political viewpoint, whatever the personal ideas of Henry III may have been — for he was scarcely an English patriot — while the economic conflicts remained subordinate to the counter-struggles of monarchies for power over disputed territories.

But there was a long way yet to go to any sense of nationality felt strongly and similarly by most members of the realm's community. Probably it was just then beginning. This may be guessed by a single odd comparison. Magna Carta was partly a penalty for John's French failure, though its text betrays no special sign of nationality. But if one compares its seventh clause, about the feudal rights of the king over the marriage of women in his gift, with the corresponding clause in the Petitions of the Barons of 1258, it will appear that at the later date the barons were asking not only that these women should not be disparaged (married off, that is, beneath their social status), but that they should not thus be given to men who were not of the nation of the kingdom of England ('*qui non sunt de natione regni Anglie*'). A little later, the Song of Lewes showed that Henry III's barons at least felt they were entitled to work out their own country's destiny with the king and without any outside help. Other popular or political poets were to take up the idea that foreigners were different, and probably unlikeable. Robert Mannyng of Brunne in 1338 remarked

> That frenche men synne yn lecherye, and englys men in envye.

Hence, the reign of Henry III was important in this development by which the politically educated classes were growing unfavourably aware of 'foreigners', the more so as Henry was himself a papally-minded king, receiving a stream of legates from Italy who were associated with assaults on the pockets of Englishmen as well as with interference in English affairs. The

21

same was true of Italian merchants and papal tax-collectors, often the same people, at a time when papal taxation of the English clergy was getting into its stride. The same again was true of Henry III's own kinsmen by marriage, the Poitevins and Savoyards who were often given favourable positions and English incomes. The movement gained strength through Edward I's foreign wars and through Edward II's predilection for Peter Gaveston who, though he may have been perfectly respectable in himself, had had the misfortune to be born a Gascon and endowed with the gift of sarcastic repartee.

Despite a dawning sense of nationality and a feeling that Englishmen were different from foreigners, especially from foreigners who came from south of the Loire, one must not antedate nationalism. The realm remained for long personified by its monarch. 'God give you victory in *your* quarrel,' cried the archers of Henry V before Agincourt.

For all that, England was coming to mean something other than the king himself. The important distinction between the king and the crown was developing. And although both Edward I and his son were allowed the principle that Gascony and Scotland were part of the realm, by 1327 the 'realm' came to mean England alone in the sense that military service outside it must be paid for.

For a long time the chivalry exemplified in Froissart and read by the aristocrats and their ladies from whom he toadied a living left a false taste of Anglo-French internationalism. For him war was a splendid game between noblemen and had little to do with the sufferings of peasants and townsmen whom the very laws of war left subject to torments unfelt by the well-horsed beholder. A similar knightly interest in the goings-on of foreign courts may be traced through the fifteenth century, whether by writers who regretted the good old days when knights had better things to do than tend their estates, or by Sir John Paston (perhaps the least realistic of his family) who liked to make wagers on whether the marriage between Charles of Burgundy and the King's sister would come off. When he had won his bet, he returned from the wedding gushingly impressed by Burgundian wealth and 'gentilesse'.* He and others went often abroad to the Low Countries, either to observe interesting sieges or to be measured for armour. The Paston household itself was one of those that kept up the demand for foreign luxuries.†

Lower down the social scale a sense of nationality and even nationalism was, however, growing stronger for a quite different reason, for here the

* *Paston Letters*, II, Nos. 574, 585.
†ibid., III, Nos. 689, 692, 728.

dislike and hatred of foreigners was becoming economic rather than political in its context. When Italian ecclesiastics came over and raised money, when foreign merchants were allowed to circumvent the customs or got the best of a bargain, it was in the last resort the English priest, artisan and tradesman who paid, even if members of the royal government sometimes felt the same animus for different reasons.

True, the French and English soldiers, mortal foes nearer home but thrown together as allies in Spain, were able to feel a certain kinship in their dangerous exile;* and there were always English merchants living abroad, like Thomas Aston, the money-lender and investor in town property, who lived in the *rue des Anglais* in Bordeaux and married a local girl. The same would be true of Calais and Bruges, to go no further.

But when things got difficult, more vivid reactions against the foreigner occurred quickly, and xenophobia, that negative but strong hallmark of nationalism, developed. The Jews, ever alien, were expelled from England in 1290 when they had served their turn and the king no longer had reason to protect them against the wrath of English debtors. Their successors as royal financiers were the Italians, privileged at the new customs barriers and ever more unpopular during the fourteenth century, as they seemed both instruments of royal financial independence and competitors for English wool. The rebels of 1381 attacked the Flemings who lived in quarters near the banks of the Thames, and in the fifteenth century the widespread loathing for foreigners, especially in London, became aggravated. German Hanseatic traders in their London 'Steelyard' were hostile agents of a Baltic trade war. Jack Cade in 1450 demanded contributions from Lombards and strangers in London and swore that otherwise his rebels would 'take the heads off as many as we can get of them'. Because Englishmen were forbidden to carry arms in Italian ports, a riot broke out in London in 1456—7 when a workman in the mercery trade saw an Italian wearing a dagger. In 1457 English shipmen – people of volatile political awareness – attacked vessels from Zeeland lying at Tilbury laden with Italian exports. The reasons for these demonstrations were complex. It was partly a demand for parity of treatment between foreigners in England and English merchants and sailors abroad; partly a fear of the French, age-old enemies on the seas and in English coastal areas where the ringing of bells habitually announced French sorties or invasion itself – a dread hardly less than that of the Scots in northern areas;

*This was said by Thomas Walsingham, monk of St Albans, in his *Historia Anglicana* (edited by H. T. Riley, Rolls Series, 1863—4, vol. 2, p. 193), under the year 1389.

partly, too, an unthinking intolerance on the part of the uneducated. But there was in addition a more reasoned economic nationalism that may have sprung from an unformulated alarm at a bad balance of payments situation; this was at any rate well exemplified in the long political poem of about 1435, entitled *The Libelle of Englyshe Polycye*.* Here was an early attempt, written by someone well informed, to show the political and commercial advantages to be gained by commanding the seas around England. It appeared at a moment when Burgundy had abandoned her alliance with England against France and the French king with Flemish support was prepared to besiege Calais. The tone is political, but the undertone is economic. The true process of English policy was summed up as

> Cherish merchandise, keep the admiralty,
> That we be masters of the narrow sea.

The author, addressing the lords of the Council, challenged a policy of mere territorial conquest and desired for reasons we might think highly intelligent 'to keep the reign at rest'. Rather than waste money on French wars we

> Might win Ireland to a full conquest
> In one sole year, to set us all in rest.

To him, sea power meant command of the waters round the British Isles, and he quotes a supposed speech made to Henry V by the Emperor Sigismund who had just visited the country and had observed, it was said, the importance of Calais and Dover.

> And to the kinge thus he said, 'My brother',
> When he perceived two towns, Calais and Dover . . .
> 'Keep these two towns sure to your majesty
> As your two eyes to keep the narrow sea!'

The greater part of the poem supplies a detailed account of the commodities and exports of various countries, from the Mediterranean to the Baltic, even including Iceland and Scotland. Protectionism and the power of blockade were alluded to, but the bitterest grievances were reserved for Venetians and Lombards whose commodities were merely 'things of complacence . . . such as suck the thrift away out of this land' —

> Apes and japes and marmusettes tailed,
> Nifles and trifles that little have availed.

The tract has an economic sophistication about it for the time, far removed

Libelle here means 'little book'.

from the brutal hostility of more emotional Englishmen, whether monks or apprentices. It called for the supervision of alien traders for clear economic reasons, and encouraged co-operation, for English benefit, with the wild Irish who nonetheless possessed a well-harboured land and the promise of fertility. Even Wales might prove a buttress and a post if the Welsh would not ally with the Scots whom everyone regarded as impossible. In the final exhortation the author wrote,

> Keep then the seas about in special,
> Which of England is the roundė wall,
> As though England were likened to a city
> And the wall environ were the sea. . . .

One cannot fail to note the resemblance to Shakespeare's later but similar encomium.

If the feeling about Italians in English court circles was liable to be cantankerous, the Italian visitor to these shores could be equally scathing, like the Venetian who wrote about 1500 that 'the English are great lovers of themselves and of everything belonging to them. They think that there are no other men than themselves, and no other world but England; and when they see a handsome foreigner they say that "he looks like an Englishman", and that "it is a great pity that he should not be an Englishman".'* Yet he granted that the English wore very fine clothes and were extremely polite in their language, which had lost the natural harshness of the German from which it was derived, and was used with great civility, the more so as the English had the habit of remaining with their heads uncovered while they talked with each other. But for all their pretty speeches, they were said to have an antipathy to foreigners.

The feelings of the populace about foreigners were cruder. In the fifteenth century English regionalism was very strong. The travel undertaken by an increasing number of people did not deter even clerks from describing Scots, Welsh and Irish as enemies of the human race. Border warfare with the Scots was continual and bestial, and, in any case, after 1378 they were looked on as schismatics because of their adherence to the French instead of to the Roman Pope. It was the same with the Irish beyond the Pale. Already under Richard II an attempt had been made to expel the Anglo-Irish in England back to their

*From *A Relation . . . of the Island of England . . . about the year 1500* made by an anonymous Italian who probably came on an embassy from Venice. It was translated by Charlotte Sneyd for the Camden Society, Old Series, No. 37 (1847), and it has been conveniently reprinted by C. H. Williams in *English Historical Documents 1485–1558*, 1967, pp. 192–201.

25

own country, and English settlers there who adopted native ways were officially described as 'degenerate'. There were many Welshmen in England, but Welsh, Irish and Scots priests were sometimes deliberately excluded by the conditions of the foundation from serving as chantry priests in the South-east. Adam of Usk, himself from the Welsh border, wrote in 1401:

... parliament ended on March 10th, and about this time ... I heard very many harsh things to be put in force against the Welsh, to wit, that they should not marry with the English, nor get them wealth nor dwell in England,

and as for Owen Glendower and his rebels, Adam described them as manni-kins (*homunculi*), emerging from caves and woods.*

The mutual antipathy felt by English, Welsh, Irish and Scots lasted through-out our period, and as late as Henry VII's reign regulations for the conduct of students at Oxford, in the college now called St Edmund's Hall, decreed that all invidious comparisons made in conversation between countries of the undergraduates' origin were to be avoided. After the battle of Wakefield, late in 1460, when Queen Margaret's men were sweeping southward, fear and dislike for northerners were naturally especially strong:

In this country [wrote Clement to John Paston] every man is well willing to go with my lords here, and I hope God shall help them, for the people in the north rob and steal, and have been appointed to pillage all this country and give away men's goods and livelihoods in all the south country, and that will ask a mischief. My lords that are here have as much as they may do to keep down all this country more than four or five shires, for it is for the well of all the south. ... †

*Adam of Usk, *Chronicon* (edited by E. M. Thompson, 1904), pp. 84, 224, 225.
†*Paston Letters*, I, No. 367.

A travelling coach, *c.* 1340. Travel was incessant.

A provincialism so strong and acrimonious might be thought to prevent any clear idea of the Englishness of Englishmen. Yet this is not so. Moments of terror are self-explanatory and prove nothing that is general. Far from a regional isolation, peaceful travel by people of all ranks even to distant parts was much more common then than is usually supposed, and with travel came not negative disgust and intolerance so much as knowledge and interest, and an enlarged sense of England's wholeness. Travellers and merchants moved about incessantly. A gild at Stratford-on-Avon, to take but one example, numbered people from London and Bristol among its members. Families like the Pastons and the Celys, whose correspondence has survived, were always making journeys from their home shires, not only to London, but recruiting servants in the west or making business voyages across the Channel. The ancient system of tolls by which towns sought to protect themselves against traders from even near-by towns had all but withered away. Clerics ran about in search of benefices and exchanged one for another quite easily, like John of Curdeswell who did not like Herefordshire, so exchanged with one Thomas who for his part wanted to leave the city of Worcester where 'the corruption of the air was bad for his complexion and because frequent incursions of his neighbours from Droitwich burdened him excessively with the expenses of food'.* Other, highly educated clerics might follow the household of a bishop in which they lived when he changed his see, like those Welshmen who came with Chichele from St David's to Canterbury and took up official positions in the church courts of the south-east. *The Canterbury Tales* show pilgrims thrown together in an atmosphere of sardonic cordiality for several days, and the same is true of pilgrims abroad, whether to Rome or to the shrine of St James of Compostella in northern Spain. Some fifteenth-century verses describe the torments of sea-sickness and how, then as now, the passengers might hope to relieve their condition by reading or querulous conversation:

> . . . som layde theyr bookys on theyr kne,
> And rad so long they myght nat se; —
> 'Allas, myne hede wolle cleve in thre',
> Thus seyth another certayne. . . .†

---

*Register of Bishop Bransford of Worcester, fo. 75v., cited by R. M. Haines, *The Administration of the Diocese of Worcester*, 1965, p. 210 n. 6.

†*The Stacions of Rome and the Pilgrims' sea voyage*, edited by F. J. Furnivall (Early Eng. Text Soc., 1867), 39.

Left Fifteenth-century pilgrims leaving Canterbury. *Above* A bookshop in early fifteenth-century England.

The flight of villeins from their manors too may be traced many miles from their former homes, and even those who stayed put were accustomed to perform carrying services or to go to market over a network of roads or along sea lanes known well enough to quite simple local people. The earliest English road map, a kind of ancestor to the AA Guide Book and called from its finder the Gough map, dates from the fourteenth century and marks in some detail the distances between towns on the major routes of the kingdom.

Leaving aside Gerald of Wales, who wrote about his Welsh and Irish itineraries in the late twelfth century and whose special aim was to further his personal ambitions, we encounter in the fifteenth century the first of the great English topographers who toured the country in a deliberate spirit of enquiry. William of Worcester was disposed to favour the aristocracy and, like his eighteenth-century successors, paid special attention to the notabilities of the regions he visited, jotting down details of their buildings and works.* But he travelled far, and wrote about what interested him in many different parts of the kingdom. He measured the church of St Mary's, Tintern, traced the sources of the Thames and Avon, assessed the value of properties in Essex, Hertford, Bristol, Southampton and Cornwall. He was curious about the nesting habits of birds and vastly interested in the islands off the coast: Ireland, the outer isles of Scotland, islands in the Bristol Channel and off the westernmost shores:

The Itinerary of William of Worcester, edited from the MS. in Corpus Christi College, Cambridge, by J. Nasmith (Cambridge, 1788).

28

The island of Caldey is a mile off the town of Tenby and measures one mile by a half, and it is peopled with thirty households, and there is a tower, and there by the shore is the chapel of St Mary and the chapel of Caldey Priory....

Or, to reproduce the flavour of his macaronic Latin:

Memorandum quod unum forland vocatum le Holyhede jacet in the west-north-west insulae de Anglesey, et est bonus portus....

William's interest in Bristol is a reminder that this flourishing port saw the busy building of ships which for their time were large and expensive, and it was the focus of an overseas exploration that was just beginning. What surer sign could there be that English identity was forming than that English mariners and traders were turning to a new and scarcely dreamed-of world? By the late fifteenth century the Germans had driven the English from the Baltic, Northern and Levantine trade were both meeting stiff competition from Italians, and so English commercial enterprise was looking for new outlets. The new competition was with the Portuguese, far to the south. Bristol customs accounts show an extensive and lucrative trade with Portugal

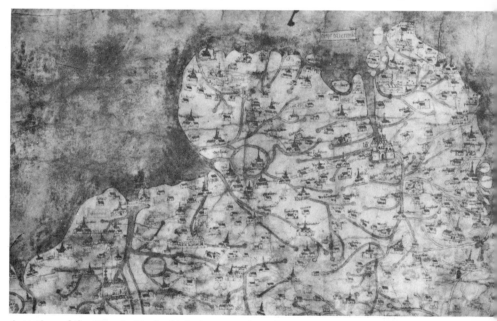

A section of the 'Gough Map' which shows roads and distances between towns in fourteenth-century England.

29

and also a rivalry with her. John Loid, master of a Bristol vessel in 1466, was later to take part in the first known English attempt to cross the Atlantic. English contacts were being made with Africa. In 1465 the King ordered payment of £48 10s. 6d. to John Lokton, draper, and Richard Whitington, also merchant of London, for buying and carrying to London from Aragon and Barbary a number of royal lions, and again in 1469 lions were being imported, though two died on the way. The records suggest regular voyages to 'Barbary' in competition with the Portuguese in the 1470s. A ship carrying English cloth touched at Madeira in 1480, and other vessels loaded sugar there. Long before the famous papal division of the western hemisphere, Edward IV was appealing to Rome to sanction English trade to Africa in order to exchange nobler for baser merchandise.

When Henry VIII was approached by the Pope to share in crusading activity in the Mediterranean, he replied that English vessels could not make the voyage past Pisa, and that England was an island concerned with its own affairs, but the excuse has a disingenuous sound, and came anyhow from a king who was able in 1533 to formulate with a new aggressiveness the idea of nationhood long and genuinely built up under his predecessors:

> This realm of England is an empire and so hath been accepted in the world ... a body politic compact of all sorts of degrees of people ... bound to bear [to him] a natural and humble obedience.*

*Preamble to the Act in Restraint of Appeals: *Statutes of the Realm*, III, p. 427.

3 The Basis of Change: the Economy

The word from which non-specialists sometimes flinch is unavoidable because the economy of late medieval England was the basis of the freshness which this book sets out to present. But the present chapter is neither a treatise nor a summary of the country's economic structure. It is intended as a sketch of change: why and how wealth was redistributed.

Admittedly, to a subject difficult enough in itself is added the confusion spread by a hundred years of controversy which began by round and contrary assertions and which is only now becoming clarified through detailed research. There is all the more reason, then, to protest with unfeigned modesty that even this sketch must be an unfinished one, erring perhaps by the drawing of erroneous conclusions and certainly by omissions.

This hundred years of debate has not yet settled the problem of the late Middle Ages. Denton's censorious picture of conspicuous lordly living alongside poverty, social disorder and unhappiness was countered by Thorold Rogers's view of a new golden age for the wage-labourer.* Even if he belonged to the old tradition of part-time scholars, Rogers was a writer who combined industry and perception, and if not all his conclusions can now be sustained, his work still stands the test of time. We must counter criticism of him by the observation that he was not trying to talk about everything at once, but that his principal thesis on wage-labourers was correct. Since his day, the attempts at synthesis which have interspersed snippets of research have sent the ball of opinion spinning now one way and now another, but this is no reason why new attempts should not be made in the interests of a lively debate in which are stimulated the pleasure of the student and the wrath of the scholar, two preconditions for keeping alive the language of

*W. Denton, *England in the Fifteenth Century* (1888), drew a depressing picture of the period, but J. E. Thorold Rogers, *Six Centuries of Work and Wages* (1884, and frequently re-edited), especially in Chapter 8, came to contrary conclusions.

historical explanation. There is, too, a certain appropriateness to our own day in fastening attention upon a past age of redistributed wealth and social mobility, if only as a consolation to some and a source of hope to others. Wealth makes free, and poverty does not ennoble unless it is personally embraced with a free will. Such problems are relevant to our own day, when redistribution appears to stimulate political and social rancour, just as it did in the late medieval period. Then also were the traditionally wealthy classes often irritated or afraid, the newly rich ambitious and hopeful, and their mutual friction often acrimonious. People who complain that there are few books in the homes of many present-day students are likely to be the same who deplore in the fifteenth century a cultural sterility and a worldly grasping after material possessions. But what else would they expect in a society where countless families were first tasting a material independence and could offer their children the only kinds of improvement they knew? If man does not live by bread alone, bread still comes first. This idea is central to the argument. It has to be set out obliquely and sometimes impressionistically, but the evidence, though scattered, seems sure. The only general concept which seems wholly false is that, still propounded by some writers of text-books, which condemns the later Middle Ages for being a remnant of days and ways that lay torpidly awaiting something entirely new. The period 1350 to 1510 was not a kind of historical fossil,

> ... the one age dead
> The other waiting to be born,

but an era of novelty behind the ancient façade.

(a) Population decline

Thomas Walsingham was an old-fashioned monk who wrote at St Albans Abbey in the late fourteenth and early fifteenth centuries. Hating change and easily excited into exaggeration and emotional disapproval, he was well enough informed to see that the plagues had made a difference.*

[In 1348] there was a great downfall of rain which lasted from midsummer till Christmas, and this was followed by mortality in the east among the Saracens and other unbelievers.... Thinking the plague had been inflicted on them for their unbelief they were converted to the faith of Christ, but when they found that the same pestilence had struck the Christian sect they returned to their vomit.... [In

*Historia Anglicana, vol. I, pp. 277–8, 409.

A physician treats a patient, Late fourteenth century.

1349] the great mortality spread throughout the world from south to north, so catastrophic that hardly half the population remained alive. Towns once full of men were left forsaken until the epidemic had left scarcely enough men alive to bury the dead. In some religious houses barely two out of twenty survived, and many folk reckon that little more than a tenth of the people were left alive. To such wretchedness succeeded [animal diseases, lack of cultivation and loss of rents] so that the world could never be the same again.

Research has confirmed the general picture, if not the details and the explanation. A recent assessment says that the Black Death of 1348—9 caused an average death-rate over England of about one third, though it was uneven in its incidence. The epidemic returned several times in the later fourteenth century, so that men could look back and calculate events by reference to the first, second or third plagues.* But as time went on and immunity was acquired by older survivors, 'the death' tended to strike the young, or to be confined to towns or particular areas. The practice of fleeing to the country became common. Oxford University dispersed frequently during the fifteenth century, and the same was true of those who could afford to do so if only they could find somewhere safe to go.

*The Register of Edmund Lacy, Bishop of Exeter, 1420—55, edited by G. R. Dunstan, Canterbury and York Society and Devon and Cornwall Record Society, Torquay, 1967, p. 217 (under the year 1440).

33

Your cousin Barney of Witchingham is passed to God, and may God cleanse him from sin [wrote Margaret to John Paston in November 1471]. Veylis' wife and Lodonys' wife are gone also. All this household and this parish are as you left them, blessed be God. We live in fear, but know not whither to flee where we can be better off than here.*

It was once thought that the death-rate from the plague was continuous enough to bring down the population without remission from 1348 until late in the fifteenth century, but more recently it has been shown that there were in fact long gaps between outbreaks which, together with their less lethal incidence, allowed momentary rises in the birth-rate. Inheritance of property moved more rapidly for obvious reasons, reduction in the number of dependants took place, and a rise in the survivors' standard of living occurred as a consequence. It is true that the worst outbreaks destroyed many potential parents. But the full effects were not felt until the later part of the century.

In this way, the plagues produced a double effect. On the one hand the later medieval world suffered in general a declining population of overall if unequal incidence, which may be proved not only by literary references and area studies, but also by the appearance of vacant land-holdings and falling agricultural prices along with the rising wages of labourers. On the other hand, the epidemics may be counted a blessing in disguise, bringing for the survivors better nutrition, the chance of earlier marriage and therefore (as the sociologists say) more marriage. Along with this went a stronger competition for women and a more civilized attitude towards them.

Such happenings were not only English. In Europe it was almost everywhere the same, and the Roman poet Francesco Berni (1469–1536) was able to compose a song on 'The Golden Days of the Plague' ('*Die goldene Pestzeit*').

No doubt the landscape looked sadder than the faces of its inhabitants. Historical investigation, which still continues, shows that this age above all was one of lost villages and depopulation. The cause was partly the plague, partly warfare, partly a flight to the towns. In Germany, the desertion of half the known sites of villages which were completely abandoned dates from the fourteenth and the fifteenth centuries. In England the same was true. Second-rate arable was abandoned. Some land was enclosed for sheep, some to make parks for the rich. The worst depopulation seems to have occurred in the inner Midland Counties, where substantial numbers of desertions appear from 1350 onwards and proliferate up to the 1480s and, at a slower rate, beyond.

Paston Letters, III, No. 681; cf. No. 680.

Disgruntled tenants sought better terms elsewhere, and as time went on it became apparent to landholders that more profit was to be had in suitable areas by turning arable over to sheep-grazing or cattle-pasture. There was in fact a curious reversal of fortunes even within the fifteenth century. In the early half at Fawsley in Northamptonshire, the Knightleys had trouble with their tenants, who found the demesne services imposed on them too irksome, but by the end of the century the boot was on the other foot, and reluctant tenants were being evicted. Eventually, the church and the great house stood alone in the parkland, and indications of former ploughlands dipped down to the edge of lakes now flooding the land of the little villages. Perhaps the site of the village lay under the water, or under the hall and its gardens. Yet here, as in other counties than Northamptonshire, there were undeserted areas where villages were not threatened by movements in the price of animal products in relation to that of cereals, and small fields were not attractive to the big graziers whose flocks ran to thousands. Or again, an agricultural area may have flourished, as we shall see, under a new kind of management.

An important consequence of the development of animal husbandry and the rise of wages appears not just in the production of more wool and leather goods which is well known, but in the higher consumption of meat by most ranks of society. Meat was demanded both by workmen in part payment for their labours and on the commercial market. In England by Richard II's reign:

> Laboreres that han no londe . to lyuen on bote here handes
> Deyned noght to dyne a-day . nyght-olde wortes.
> May no peny-ale hem paye . ne a pece of bacon,
> Bote hit be fleesch other fysch . fried other ybake,
> And that *chaud* and *pluschaud* . for chillyng of here mawe.*

In Alsace, servants of husbandry had to be given at harvest time so much meat that the slices 'hung over the plate'. Cattle were imported into Germany from Denmark and eastern Europe, especially Hungary. In the Odenwald, labourers in 1483 insisted on meat and wine twice a day as part of their wages. Demands like this could be met by the raising of sheep whose wool was needed for cloth and of cattle for the leather industries, the products of which themselves could now be afforded by more people. An interesting comparison has been made between the standard of living of workers in the fifteenth century and at about 1900, and it has been shown to be much the

*The Vision of Piers the Plowman, B Text, Passus VI, lines 309–13.

same in respect of food, save that the best protein in the form of meat and fish was eaten at the earlier time.

In London, stricter regulation of the meat trade was being enforced in the later fourteenth century when consumption of animals rose and high production on farms linked to metropolitan butchery interests created problems about the disposal of offal. Contrary to general belief, public sentiment was strongly against throwing stinking rubbish into public sewers, and butchers had to organize special shambles (abbatoirs), for instance at Queenhithe, where muck was to be rowed into mid-stream and dumped at ebb-tide. In 1402 a pier was built off Pudding Lane for the Eastcheap butchers.

(b) The puzzle of poverty

From what has been said, there might be reason enough to think of later medieval Europe, including England, as an impoverished world compared with that of the thirteenth century when new and magnificent buildings arose in profusion (at the expense of the poor) and civilization flourished; or compared again with the sixteenth century when a new civilization (again at the expense of the poor) asserted itself. Economic historians of great distinction have written about the later Middle Ages as a time of contracted economy. In a certain sense it is impossible to contradict them. The French have not unnaturally tended to blame the war for decimating the country, slowing production and exchange, and bringing in its wake exhausting taxes. Indeed, medieval men were not accustomed to taxation as we are today and did not allow for it in their private budgets. John Beele of Sevenoaks in 1472 was doubtless not unique when he left, as a charitable bequest, the yearly profit of a house and garden for poor men of the parish 'att such tyme as ther shalbe anny taxe tallage or fifteenth axed or levied for the kyng'.* In the same vein, John Paston wrote to his brother in London in 1473, just when a new French expedition was being prepared:

I pray God send you the Holy Ghost among you in the parliament house, and rather the Devil, we say, than you should grant any more taxes....†

Much direct taxation disappeared into the pockets of assessors and collectors. One way out of this difficulty was to impose levies on transactions of goods, like wool, leather or salt. A customs system became regular in England under

*Somerset House, Prerogative Court of Canterbury Will Register 'Wattys', folios 64–5.
†*Paston Letters*, iii, No. 720.

Edward I, and indirect taxation was elaborated with mediocre success in fourteenth-century France. But such devices meant higher prices, and in any case the incidence of war taxation discouraged demand and damped down production.

An uncertain system of regular taxation likewise means that government credit becomes bad. Anyone with a bank account today knows that it is easier to borrow on overdraft if income is steady and reliable, and the lesson is no less true for medieval rulers who often had to finance themselves by borrowing on the security of taxes that were yet to come in. If direct taxation produced too little (as it did), and indirect taxation was too often assigned away to royal creditors, borrowing conditions became heavy and royal treasuries became encumbered with debts which could be repaid only with difficulty, if at all. The weakness of later medieval monarchies sprang in no small measure from this failure of credit. Money became dear. Kings might save themselves for a time by devaluation of the currency, but this disguised form of bankruptcy is harmful to strong and confident government.

Some historians also blame a decline in the actual amount of money available when they explain national impoverishment, arguing that the production of silver fell off as mines could no longer be fully exploited until technical changes had solved the problems of deep-level drainage. Gold was too valuable to be a convenient medium for small transactions, and anyhow fetched a better price on the bullion market than at the mints, so that gold coins tended to go out of circulation. Shortage of bullion led to hoarding, either by hiding precious metal in treasuries or by using it in the form of fine gold and silver utensils and jewelled settings, and thus by a vicious circle the hoarding was perpetuated and aggravated. The war between England and France also contributed to periods of cash scarcity, since embargoes on the Anglo-Flemish trade in wool interrupted the flow of payments. Government orders that money coming into the Staple at Calais should be mostly returned to England were resisted. In 1390 the chronicler Knighton, writing in Leicester, described a great scarcity in England, when he saw children crying with hunger in the streets, not because the harvest had failed but because there was no cash available to buy food while the wool, which should have been sold, lay in English warehouses and its export was forbidden by statute.* There is also a relationship in time between moments of such scarcity of bullion and complaints

*Henry Knighton, canon of Leicester, *Chronicon* (edited by J. R. Lumby, Rolls Series, vol. II, 1895), pp. 314—15.

in Parliament that money was being drained away out of the kingdom. This too was one of the difficulties which increased Englishmen's dislike of foreigners, especially Italians, whom they accused of carting off vast sums to their own land.

Where French scholars have paid more attention to war and fiscal crisis in accounting for late medieval 'contraction' and decline, Englishmen have tended to blame the Black Death, and it is hard not to agree that as the population grew smaller more land was withdrawn from cultivation and landlords were burdened with lapsed or lowered rents. The age is seen as one of gloom for landlords. A principal author of this view, Professor Postan, has more recently felt obliged to counter a new argument, that the long war with France enriched Englishmen at French expense by bringing loot and ransoms into their hands and French territory under English exploitation.* After all, war itself is an unproductive activity. It takes men who can ill be spared away from field and workshop, or at best sets them to the production of munitions which are by their very nature wasteful. It is true that French noblemen brought high ransoms to England when they were captured and had to be redeemed by their French dependants, but the reverse is also true, and Englishmen were equally liable to capture and to pay for their losses in men and materials. A few war profiteers may have made good. But the country as a whole had to raise some £8¼ million as taxation for the Hundred Years War, of which half came from the taxation of wool, and by no means all of this was borne by the foreign buyer. English economic activity as a whole suffered, and those who profited, far from investing in recovery, used their wealth in traditional ways to enhance their social position, buying property in the countryside without really improving it, and spending money on extravagant clothing and articles of luxury which often enough came from abroad.

For such reasons it is doubtful if the view of national impoverishment can be upset. There was a decline in the total amount of wealth produced – in the 'Gross National Product' – which was not offset either by new investment or by new techniques of production.

Yet a puzzle of poverty remains, if one sets out from these convictions in search of the poor themselves. Needless to say, there are in every society some poor who are always with us, whether they be widows, the old, the half-witted or the professional 'layabouts'. A Wycliffite writer alluded to

*M. M. Postan, 'The Costs of the Hundred Years War', *Past and Present*, No. 27, 1964, pp. 34–53.

Christ's commandment to give alms to 'pore feble men, to pore croked men, to pore blynde men, and to bedraden men'.* Fourteenth-century French and English painting depicts beggars in the streets.† When in 1397 the earl of Arundel was taken to execution, a sorrowful chronicler tells how he distributed alms to beggars sitting by the roadside between Westminster Palace and Charing Cross.‡ In countless wills, bequests are made to poor men, or bedridden men — the equivalent of our pensioners — and to poor maidens who hoped for dowries to improve their chances on the marriage market. In 1388 the Cambridge parliament legislated for the first time against sturdy beggars who would not work, a section of society more familiar to students of Tudor times when the situation had changed. But this has reference to agricultural labourers on the run from their native manors in search of higher wages, not to men for whom there was no work at all.§

*The Vision of Piers the Plowman, edited by W. W. Skeat, vol. II (1886), 113.
†The Flowering of the Middle Ages, edited by Joan Evans (1966), pp. 20–21.
‡Annales Ricardi Secundi (edited by H. T. Riley, Rolls Series, 1866), 216.
§Knighton, Chronicon, II, p. 303.

Left Leprous beggar-woman of fourteenth-century England. Right Rich and poor: a fifteenth-century illustration of the parable of Dives and Lazarus.

More difficult is the problem of the landlord whose rent-roll shrank as his costs rose, his labourers disappeared, and his need to maintain display and conspicuous living remained. There is evidence for a landlord problem in England, France and Germany. Professor Postan found lower profits in over 400 of 450 manors he studied. Few will argue that lease prices did not decline over most of England in the earlier and middle fifteenth century. M. Boutruche has seen a sorry state of affairs in the vineyards of the Bordelais, ravaged by troops and neglected by lords who hardly knew where their loyalties lay. Professor Abel in Germany found that prices for arable leases in Göttingen declined by two thirds between 1431 and 1500, and repeated as an example the complaints of the Saxon knight in 1474 whose livelihood depended on continuing his hop-garden, yet had to pay more for hop-poles and for the labour which was needed to train the plants on them, however uncertain the harvest.

In spite of all this, there are some contrary indications. The real money income of the Archbishop of Canterbury appears to have remained stable throughout the fifteenth century, and rose after 1475, as a decline in some parts of his enormous and scattered estates was offset by good prices for rich leases in east Kent and in the regions near London. Not long ago, a short book by Dr A. R. Bridbury appeared with the paradoxical title: *Economic Growth: England in the later Middle Ages*, in which he claimed that despite the fourteenth-century population loss, fifteenth-century England showed 'an astonishing record of resurgent vitality and enterprise', that tin production was buoyant and cloth export unaffected till 1400, when it fell only in proportion to the fall in population, and even then maintained its monetary value while home consumption kept pace with exports into the bargain.

Several answers may be suggested to this apparent contradiction between sad decay and fresh vitality. The principal one is that a decline in gross national product does not necessarily imply individual poverty if production per head is maintained or raised. There is no reason why this should not have been so. If there are fewer people to share what has been produced, each may, in simple arithmetical terms, be as rich as before. Secondly, it may well be wrong to treat the period 1350 to 1510 as all of a piece, since moments of depression during a century and a half can give a false impression, the more so in an age when bad harvests, periods of bad weather, and years of unprofitable warfare could cause a suffering temporary in itself but expressed with misleading violence in partial statistics or literature. Thirdly, different regions of the country could well receive different experiences, so that the decline of one town might run parallel with the rise of a new locality, a large estate might be broken only to emerge as a series of flourishing small estates with scanty records, or as pasture flourished while poor arable stayed untilled. Finally, there is a reasoned case for the redistribution of wealth in England itself, partly as possession spread downwards, and partly as one geographical area benefited while another did not. It seems sensible, then, to abandon any attempt to write about English prosperity or poverty as a whole, and to turn instead to changes in the country between regions and classes, and the rates of these changes.

(c) The geographical distribution of wealth in England
There are enough useful records of taxation in England to show how the distribution of taxable wealth in 1334 compared with that at the beginning of the sixteenth century. Research on the subject is highly technical, but a number of broad conclusions emerge, especially from the work of Mr R. S. Schofield.* In the first place, the assessed taxable wealth of the country as a whole increased on average about threefold within this period. This takes into consideration the fact that the prices of consumer goods were roughly at the same level at the two dates. Even if some caution is needed in accepting this increase, and even if there were many people whose incomes were too low to bring them within the tax-paying classes, such a result is sufficiently remarkable for an age of supposed decline, and suggests in itself a wider distribution of wealth. Apart from this, it is evident that taxable wealth was spreading eastwards and southwards. In 1334 the poorest county was Lancashire, the richest were Kent and the midland counties which stretched in a narrow band from Gloucestershire and Wiltshire north-eastwards to East Anglia and the East Riding of Yorkshire. To see this matter another way, if we leave aside small areas of specially marked wealth, the twelve richest counties almost exactly comprised the midland belt bounded on the south-east by a line from Reading to Yarmouth. The further one moved away from this belt, the poorer the country became, and the north-west contained most of the poorest counties of all.

In 1515 the range of wealth was much wider. Lancashire and the north-west were still the poorest regions, but the wealthier ones now comprised all England south of a line drawn between the Wash and the Severn. Exceptional

---

*This paragraph is much indebted to R. S. Schofield, 'The Geographical Distribution of Wealth in England, 1334–1649', in the *Economic History Review*, Second Series, vol. XVIII, No. 3, December 1965, pp. 483–510.

A fifteenth-century impression of London.

wealth lay in two well-defined areas: Gloucestershire, Somerset and Wiltshire; and (if a London historian may be forgiven the phrase) the home counties.

London itself, already much richer in 1334 than the rest of the country, had by 1515 become richer still in proportion. In 1334 it accounted for 2 per cent of the assessed (non-ecclesiastical) wealth of the country. In 1515 it accounted for nearly 9 per cent. London, indeed, had continued, since long before the period covered by this book, to grow in population and activity as the capital of the country, where the permanent courts of justice and government were housed, where great men of all kinds possessed town houses, merchants dwelt and worked, and whither young men went in search of common-law training by which to make a prestigious living and to defend their family's property through litigation, and to seek marriageable women as wives.

During the later Middle Ages there had also been a high rate of wealth increase in the south-western peninsula and in the block of counties round London, where shipping and the cloth industry flourished and where the recovery of population levels pushed up rents.

In general, it was a story not unfamiliar today, of a drift to the south. In particular, the south-east and the south-west were pulling even further ahead of the north.

Left Carpenter and mason.
Above Building works.

A master-mason consults the King. Fourteenth-century England.

(d) The towns

This change in the location of wealth over England as a whole was partly caused by the rise of some urban areas and the decline of others. Places which had been famous and flourishing in the thirteenth century were sometimes in a poor state by the fifteenth. Londoners who wanted to get rid of the hated Venetians, Genoese and Florentines could think of no worse fate for them short of shutting them up in castles than to send them to Winchester, where grass grew in the streets and the churches were decayed. Empty houses lay behind the city walls of Oxford. Lincoln as a notable cloth-making town — Lincoln Green — was giving place to other centres.

These shifts were not to be seen in England alone. The population of north German cities had declined by about 20 per cent during our period, and similar contractions happened in Bordeaux, Toulouse, Rouen, Arras, Metz and the ancient textile centres of Ypres and Ghent. Bruges was silting up and new activity was replacing it further north, in Antwerp and Brabant.

44

One of the verbose Italian visitors to England at the end of the period thought that only Bristol and York were worth speaking of outside London. He wrote with a confident exaggeration not unusual in foreign sightseers. It is remarkable what fascination York had for them. None the less, the case of York is an interesting one because it illustrates both rise and decline within the fourteenth and fifteenth centuries and is a reminder that the English universe did not revolve around London alone. York was, and remained, one of England's leading cities, but for reasons which changed. It was a frontier town, as it had been in Roman days: a military, administrative and social centre. Sometimes the court and even the Exchequer moved there when an expedition against the Scots was being undertaken. Northern gentry came thither for social life, sometimes marrying into leading city families. Churches, especially those of the ever-popular Franciscan and Dominican friars, received bequests, and the future Pope Pius II marvelled at the minster with its slender columns and vast windows. Produce was distributed through its market, bows were made, bells founded, and its pewter was second in repute only to that of London. The governing class was recruited largely from men who had made their fortunes in foreign trade. Yet although York maintained a certain pre-eminence, it began to be affected not only by the decline in overseas commerce but by the change in location of later medieval England's most vital industry — cloth.

The same was happening to Oxford, Winchester and Lincoln, whose decay has been noted, and to other places where clothworkers were growing few and impoverished. For as the mechanical felting of cloth by means of water-driven fulling mills spread, so too the manufacture of textiles moved from their older centres to country areas where there were swift streams to drive the hammers. Here cheaper cloth could be produced with rural labour, to satisfy a heightened local demand. Here too there could be an air of freedom from established municipal restrictions. The day of the West Riding of Yorkshire was dawning. Durham Abbey began to buy its cloth from men in Halifax and Leeds instead of York; and York tailors took to stocking country cloth. For the same reason Suffolk and the Waveney valley became important. Thomas Spring III of Lavenham grew to be one of the richest men outside London other than members of the peerage. The same was true of Wiltshire and the Cotswold country where fulling mills were built along streams that descended the little valleys. The atmosphere of these places can still be captured by anyone who takes a walk through Bradford-on-Avon or the more beautiful Castle Combe where the lane through the village and its mellowed houses leading up the tree-lined road still looks down on

Water-mill. Fifteenth-century France.

the fast stream intersected by dams. Coventry throve on wool and cloth-making, and was full of mercers and drapers. Dyers who set up in these little industrial complexes were men as stubborn as weavers long ago had been, combining in 1415 to raise the price of dyeing, in 1475 to make their own regulations, and in 1490 refusing to join in the pageant of Corpus Christi Day. To such places came orders for liveries, or uniforms, placed by social leaders like Sir John Fastolf for his men. Norfolk worsteds too were still in demand: in 1465 there was a month's delay in the delivery of fine worsted,* and in the cold autumn of that year John Paston asked Margaret to send him two 'cloves' of worsted for doublets, and to find out where William Paston bought his own fine worsted 'which is almost like silk' and to buy some even if it were more expensive, 'for I would make my doublet all worsted for worship of Norfolk'.† On such trade clothiers grew rich, filling their fine houses, newly built, with silver and employing as labourers weavers and (in the case of felted cloth) fullers, who themselves grew well-to-do and stimu-lated a local market in food and strong drink.

The swing of economic fortune that brought greater wealth to the east and the south of the country, emphasizing home industry at the expense of foreign trade, especially with northern Europe, affected also the shipping industry. It has already been seen how Bristol was engaged in building large

* *Paston Letters*, II, No. 529.
†ibid., No. 528.

Top left Sheep-shearing. Fifteenth century. *Above left* Flemish dyers, 1482. *Above right* Weaving on a hand-loom. Fifteenth-century Flanders. *Below* The master of the Wool Staple holds an interview.

vessels and undertaking the first voyages to Africa and into the further western seas. A rather different development affected the shipping of the eastern coast. In the late Middle Ages the coastal districts of the east from Berwick to the Thames contained about half of the most populous and thriving towns of the kingdom. As foreign trade fell off, inshore trade developed, based on regional capitals like Hull and Newcastle, and supporting the shipping and economies of a multitude of little creeks and havens. Food was exchanged for small quantities of wine and luxuries. Yarmouth and Lynn provided food both for the north and for the ever-growing London market. A vital and expanding trade was in coal, brought from the Tyne southwards. In distinction from the large ships of the west, this coal, iron and food were conveyed along the eastern shores by quite small vessels which rarely exceeded 100 tons. The economy demanded short runs into bad harbour approaches, and large ships were difficult to freight, slow and needed a disproportionately large crew. In general, shipping, which was part of industrial life, was now largely in English hands, a fairly large employer of wage-labour, and contributed a good proportion of the country's industrial capital. In such vessels the traditions of naval command and administration were being learned which later would stand England in good stead.

Left Flemish ships of *c.* 1500. *Right* Iron-miner of the Forest of Dean in fifteenth-century England.

Fifteenth-century blacksmith.

One more fresh development to which allusion has been made was in coal mining. Durham Cathedral accounts take notice of mining activities, and the urbanization of the countryside owed something at this stage to coal as well as to cloth. The lucky survival of a Durham iron-master's weekly accounts from 1409 provides a detailed picture of the building of a new forge and its equipment. It was called 'Byrkeknott' and possibly corresponds to Bedburn Forge in Weardale. The forge lay at a little distance from a marshy stream, and several wooden houses were built in the clearing. The forge itself was of timber, roofed with turf. It possessed a furnace for smelting and another for the subsequent working of the iron. The stream was dammed and the water led by an artificial channel of stone and wood. A charcoal burner was employed by the bishop to convert his wood into charcoal, a bloomsmith had charge of the smelting, a *faber* worked over the iron and cut it into suitable pieces for transport and sale to local smiths. The whole forge was producing about two tons a week. Perhaps it was such a factory that kept a fifteenth-century poet awake at night and formed the subject-matter of an early English lyric:

> Swarte-smeked smethes, smatered with smoke,
> Drive me to deth with den of here dintes:
> Swich nois on nightes herd men never,
> What knaves cry and clattering of knockes. . . .*

It was no rural blacksmith that kept the writer in furious wakefulness, but a profit-making concern on overtime.

* *Medieval English Lyrics*, edited by R. T. Davies (1963), 213.

(e) The countryside

Characteristic of later medieval England is the interpenetration of town and country life. All towns, save perhaps London, wore a countrified air, barns and granaries opening off the streets as in a Kate O'Brien novel. Most were without suburbs, as in Hardy's Casterbridge, where a field labourer could toss a stone through the window of the clerk standing at his desk. The other side of the coin is the countryside injected with new life, attractive to speculators, tenant-farmers and small traders, who penetrated and broke down the great old estates into smaller, more independent units which, for all that, were filled with vitality and enterprise. Successful businessmen can be found in plenty, in a modest way compared with those of Lombardy or the Low Countries. But they formed no stable patrician class in the sense that particular families retained a great dominance over the generations, and it was a common thing for a successful merchant to have come from the country, see his son at the height of urban fortune, perhaps as mayor, and his grandson return to the country more affluent than himself. 'From clogs to clogs in three generations' is a good enough saying, save that the grandson's shoes were doubtless better than clogs. It would perhaps be better to say, as Tudor people did, that 'every gentleman flyeth unto the country'. England was still an agricultural nation. The dynasties of even London merchants were short-lived, and trade and commerce relied upon a supply of outsiders, whether apprentices from the shires, well enough connected to get a foothold in the city, or land-owning and eligible men who sought mercantile daughters and widows as wives to bolster their fortunes. The intermixture

of bourgeois and gentleman, rustic and town-worker, proceeded without difficulty and was creating a new middle class. It is worth remembering that at the beginning of the fourteenth century the parliamentary knights felt themselves more at one with the lords, while at the end of that century knights and burgesses met and talked together at the time of parliament, forming a body that could justly be called the Commons, far grander than the commons in the universal sense of the English people, yet coherent and lesser than the lords of parliament who still ruled the country.

There is another side to the relationship between town and country. Today we are all familiar with the longing for country life. As the fields and the woods were tamed into safety and communication became adequate to supply the wants of townsmen, and as towns became increasingly unpleasant to live in, so there developed an attitude to the country which was partly utilitarian (fresh air, sound investment, and freedom from gild restrictions) and partly romantic (the idyll of rural life and the dignified independence felt even by a freehold cottager). This 'pastoralism' was becoming evident in the later Middle Ages. At the highest level it can be seen in the growing number of licences from the King for great men to impark land, or even crenellate their houses, less as fortification than as an exterior symbol of grandeur. Financial accounts of great estates sometimes show that the deer parks were uneconomic and had to be subsidized from manorial profits or rents derived elsewhere, but they gave prestige and pleasure in safe and fashionable hunting, the supply of upper-class foods like venison and a score of varieties

Left Ploughing in fifteenth-century Flanders. The ploughman was still a symbolic figure of Everyman. *Right* A fifteenth-century barn. 'Tho were faitours a-fered and flowen to Peersses bernes. . .' (*Vision of Piers the Plowman*, C, IX, 179).

Above House of the wool merchant, William Grevel, at Chipping Camden, in the Cotswolds. *Opposite page* Cloth merchant's house at Coggeshall, Essex, built on the fortune of Thomas Paycocke after his death in 1461.

of birds, and the opportunity for high-level converse and decisions which today would like as not be made on the golf-course. Nor, as so often happened on the Continent, did great *rentiers* run away to town and forget about their country estates at court or on campaign. No century before the fifteenth saw such skilled and elaborate professional organization for the regular maintenance of leased land, repairs to roofs and hedges, arrangements for the lord's transport system of horse stabling, or the proper occupation of his manorial buildings by lessees who would reside and 'make neither strip nor waste'. London was becoming more and more unpleasant. There were squalid slums where workers in light metals lived, making pins and spurs in teeming tenements. Smoke from wood and now coal in breweries and workshops had begun to pollute the atmosphere. Plague was widely seen as an urban disease, and those who could afford to do so fled from the scene of epidemics. Real property in the home counties was becoming a good investment, for it did not sink like venturing ships nor default like debtors, it could easily be sold or mortgaged or leased if cash were needed, and it could produce at least a steady and often satisfactory income from rents. All the letter-writing families — Pastons, Celys, Stonors and Plumptons —joined in this game. When Geoffrey Chaucer was doing well in his career, he bought himself a place in Greenwich, of which he wrote with tender satisfaction:

52

Hoom to myn hous ful swiftly I me spedde;
And, in a little erber that I have,
Y-benched newe with turvės fresshe y-grave
I bad men shulde me my couchė make. . . . *

Furthermore, if you take a section of contemporary wills made by better-off Londoners and men from south-eastern England, and plot on a map the residences of testators who had some cause to be near London, you will have to make a thick rash of dots in the region of Greenwich and Deptford, then open to the sky and popular with the prosperous.

What is true of towns and their penetration by country-born people is true also in reverse. There was much social mobility in the geographical sense, much penetration of the countryside by urban, trade and industrial development. Something of this has already been seen, and there will be more to be said later.

For all this, England was still primarily rural in aspect, and it is right to pay a little attention to the different kinds of estates that covered the country. Foremost were the big landlords, some lay and some ecclesiastical, rooted in the soil and deriving their status and quality from it. The western midlands were long dominated by the earls of Warwick and the lords of Berkeley, whose 'castle' remains today as one of the most perfect examples of fortified

*The Legend of Good Women, Text A, Prologue, lines 96–9.

living. In the same area the priory and cathedral of Worcester as church lords dominated the scene. In the south-east, the cathedral and archbishopric of Canterbury had no rivals as lords whose power was exercised in scores of country courts and prevailed over the activities of lesser men. Lords tried to influence the choice of parliamentary knights, sometimes successfully. Knights, esquires, gentlemen and yeomen could be ordered at short notice to be ready and 'defensibly arrayed' by messengers who gave them a rendezvous when a political situation became urgent. Yet no areas were held in great force. The private castles on which the higher nobility spent so much were scarcely ever held against an enemy. War interfered little with the normal pursuits of hunting and outdoor enjoyment, litigation and local feuding. Many individuals who fought in the civil wars were richer than their fellows, but it is hard to argue from this any assiduous cultivation of rural wealth in society's higher echelons. Infertility, disease, and political fortunes and misfortunes served among the lay aristocracy especially to redistribute wealth and regroup estates in the hands of new families.

Lower down the social scale the fifteenth century brought more noticeable changes. By the 1370s and 1380s great lords in most places were finding it an insupportable burden to administer the old 'manorial system', so often and wrongly thought of as typical of the whole Middle Ages. It was difficult when the price of produce was low to pay for a whole system of bailiffs, reeves and servile workers. In the thirteenth century the story had been quite different: a bulging population, many mouths to feed and hence a demand for grain; many arms eager and even desperate for work. Landlords could take their profit then, not ploughing it back into better production to raise standards all round, but investing it for their own ends and, if they were churchmen, raising enormous buildings to the glory of God and of themselves in unguessable proportions. But now labour was hard to get: expensive if it had to be bought, and unobtainable if the old cheap labour services were demanded. Men simply ran away. So owners of great estates took to leasing out the good lands which since about 1200 they had kept 'in demesne' for their own exploitation and profit. This leasing took place at different times and speeds according to the estate and locality. But it began in real earnest in the late fourteenth century and was pretty well complete by the mid fifteenth. Those who took up these leases were often at first the reeves or more distinguished of the erstwhile peasantry, who chose to take on the demesnes, or parts of them, for a shortish term of years and get what they could out of them for a fixed annual rent. Sometimes even whole groups of peasants can be found as lessees. But before long others joined in, and gentry, yeomen, merchants and husbandmen can be found as lessees, for lengthening periods and at modest rents. These people had a fair amount of freedom now that more land per head was available. They could choose what they would or would not take. They were not bound to any particular lord for their leased lands but could look round the market, strike bargains, offer resistance to pressure, and use their wits to invest and cultivate. They could raise sheep if the area was suitable, as in eastern Kent. Or they could grow grain on the better lands, hiring labour as they could afford it, often working with their own hands too, and submitting only to the agreed contract about upkeep of buildings, fences and tilth. If such a lessee – or 'farmer' (*firmarius*), as he was called – agreed to do all the maintenance, his annual rent would be lower than if the lord were bound to look to the roofs and fences.

In this way, rural estates which once had been huge and cumbersome often became reorganized into smaller and shifting units. Stylized manorial account documents do not often afford much information of these changes, but they were there none the less, and are demonstrated in great numbers of wills, deeds and contemporary letters, which reinforce what we can learn by close inspection of the traditional lordly documents. The lessees were the real new lords of the land – the 'gentlemen and thrifty and substantial yeomen' and 'thrifty husbandmen, and the franklins and good men' of the Paston letters.* In August 1456 Lord Scales fixed a business meeting for the 19th of the month, but supposed that 'learned men will not be easy to get because of the busy time of harvest',† and we even hear of an Oxford coroner, a royal official of some local standing, trudging at the plough-tail. The Pastons themselves were rather grander than this and one of them expressed the hope that the younger sons would not have to hold the plough. But at least they could contemplate it. Such men were both landlords and workers, operating on a system more flexible than the older one of great and undivided estates, but deeply concerned with their profits and the leases they might sell or buy. Contemporary correspondence is full of such negotiations, showing anxiety for the upkeep of leased land, advertising farms to let, jumping at the opportunity of a good lease, with preference for their kinsmen if the writer himself did not want to buy,‡ and doing all possible to gather in the rents from their own lessees when they fell due. In 1461 the Paston's

---

Paston Letters I, Nos. 180, 361.
†ibid. No. 292.
‡ibid. No. 183.

bailiff, Richard Calle, was 'walking about all the lordships and speaking with the farmers and tenants to understand their dispositions and receive money from them', finding them well disposed towards John Paston, and getting them to agree to pay over the rents only to him (for there was some dispute about possession), and in return he guaranteed to 'see them harmless'.* Unreliable farmers were to be avoided.†

In a system of land investment which was, after all, becoming very complex, it would be surprising not to find that the equivalent of modern estate agents existed, and the Paston Letters offer some slight evidence that members of the clergy could act in this capacity, just as religious houses acted as deposit bankers.‡

It is clear that the men who took on leases and became tenant farmers were themselves of differing status. Their fortunes are hard to follow because they kept few records. Probably, in fact, it was part of their economic strength *not* to employ a large accounting apparatus like a great lord who needed an audit at least once a year. Most farmers' writings were confined to deeds of acquisition and sale. But these they treasured very carefully. Margaret Paston told her son that his father 'set more store by his writing and evidence than he did by any movable goods', and that if he lost these he could not get them again.§ It was a litigious age. To a gentleman, however, household accounts too were of the highest value, and had to be properly audited, for otherwise he could not easily know what he might spend outside, nor 'whether he go backwards or forwards'. ‖ Yet not all farmers were gentlemen. Broadly speaking, it seems that the later one goes into the fifteenth century, the more distinguished and 'gentle' the farmer was likely to be. But leaving this aside, there were periods, especially in the middle of the century, when leases were hard to sell because the economic climate was not good, while later in the century conditions improved, contracts for longer periods were made, and the farmed areas became larger. All this time, the farmer of any given estate might be a gentleman or a yeoman or a husbandman. Gentlemen were becoming more interested, but the last two classes were improving themselves, too, and it is, in fact, not easy to tell the difference between a yeoman and a husbandman. A given man might be called by several descriptions. In eastern Kent at the end of our period the biggest and dearest leases

Paston Letters II, No. 418; cf. 420, 438.
†ibid. No. 447.
‡ibid., I, Nos. 153, 183, 380, etc.; II, Nos. 556, 561, 647.
§ibid. II, No. 560; cf. III, No. 670.
‖ ibid. I, Nos. 304, 305.

were usually held by 'yeomen', and sometimes a yeoman's family history may be traced over the centuries as, like the Knatchbulls (nickname for butcher), they progressed through gentility to knighthood and even the peerage. The Knatchbulls became Lords Brabourne in 1880, possessing over 4,000 acres in that part of Kent where they began their recorded history. A lesser family were the Halls, yeomen of Bexley, whose testaments show them anxious about upkeep and the continuous dwelling of their heirs upon their land. They left animals and grain to their survivors and servants as well as money and clothes; their debts were to be paid promptly, the widows were to have their dower, the children and charities their share.*

Away in Caernarvonshire, no less than in Kent, gentry like Bartholomew Bolde can be discovered buying up parcels of land in the early fifteenth century and amassing a family property composed of hundreds of acres of arable and thousands of pasture, the possession of which was continued under his son-in-law, William Bulkeley. Today a leading hotel in Beaumaris is called the Bulkeley Arms.

For all the wills and deeds that remain, the hardest task is to scrutinize the texture of the late medieval countryside. How did men of small and middling means work and live? Only samples from diverse sources can at present suggest the answer, and the answer is obviously manifold. In the pastoral north, where men 'knew no prince but a Percy', life was rougher than in the south. Peasant houses were small, either one- or two-roomed cottages, or long houses where cattle and human beings dwelt under the same roof though separated by a cross-passage, and perhaps built with stone foundations and even stone walls. In the south, lessees were likely to have possessed themselves of some of the old manorial buildings of stone or wood or even brick, dwelling with their indoor servants, sleeping in feather beds, living among colourful hangings and the pewter-ware off which they ate a good protein diet. But we cannot know much of the poorer people's mode of life, save that they were cramped into cottages and mean little dwellings, provided sometimes with chimneys but often unglazed and protected against wind and rain by opaque window coverings.

The countryside was certainly penetrated by tradesmen who catered for tastes that could now be more widely afforded. By the fifteenth century it is not easy to tell a man's trade by his 'surname'. Trade names had the habit of

---

*The will of Thomas Hall (1526) is in Somerset House, register 'Porch', folio 20; that of William Hall (1512) is a rare example of a will in Somerset House which is not registered but is filed loose.

clinging, even to men who had left their former avocation, or adopted more than one. A husbandman of Kent was keeper of the king's castle in Canterbury; a yeoman of Herne was said to 'go about his business of labouring as a husbandman'; another husbandman was also a butcher, and another a sawyer. Of two brothers from Hartfield in Sussex, one was a husbandman, the other was called a common labourer. All these examples are from the early 1450s.* The line between craftsmen, traders and agriculturalists was a fluid one. Quite sophisticated trades, too, can be found in small villages, not only of the ubiquitous butcher, poulterer, baker and brewer, but the spicer in Sutton Valence and the pepperer in Brenchley.

Essex and East Anglia formed another area where society was in a state of dissolution and re-establishment. Villeins ran away to towns and set up on their own at a distance of ten, twenty or thirty miles, becoming independent and earning relatively high wages, whether in woodcutting at Thaxted, maltmongering, navigating ships or catching oysters. If they stayed in agriculture they sought employment with the new leaseholders, demanding good wages and food. They might travel about, especially at harvest time, looking for lucrative employment as reapers and threshers, very like the characters in Thomas Hardy's *Mayor of Casterbridge*. Wealth came in occasional odd ways, too; perhaps from the French war, as in 1449 when a brewer of Sandwich called John Carter (note the different names) had a royal passport (for which he must have paid) which allowed him to take ship for Picardy and there collect the ransom money of eight marks (£5 6s. 8d.) upon which a captured French knight's family had agreed with two east Kentish villagers into whose hands the unfortunate knight had fallen. Fraudulent conversion by this middleman brought the case into the King's Bench, but it illustrates a war enterprise which had its small investors and an organization that existed for the realization of such profits.†

Life such as this was not lived by classes in isolation. Great and small needed each other. At Peterborough there was a great variety of trades, dominated perhaps by the carpenter to whom the fifteenth-century standard of living owed so much though so obscurely. But Peterborough's economic life was borne along on a vast and continuous network of credit transactions. The Abbey's almoner kept an account book recording loans to individuals of every station and profession. Many lowly men and women owed small sums for their rent, for grain, malt and firewood. More substantial merchants

Kent Records (Kent Archaeological Society), vol. XVIII, 1964, pp. 220–65.
†ibid., 241.

owed the almoner money too, and often bought from him meat, grain, hay and timber, or sold him spices and wine. They could expect to receive and give credit for a year or more. At regular intervals the mutual debts were set off against each other and the net balance was either settled in cash or carried over for another term. The situation must have been not unlike that produced by the bank strike in Ireland in 1966, when cheques were freely exchanged between traders in return for goods, and exchanged again for cash with anyone who happened to have a supply at hand, so that despite an obstruction in the supply of new money, a circulation of old money could be maintained, supported by a basic confidence and a minimal amount of book-keeping. The almoner of Peterborough's account book is also a reminder that money-lending was freely practised in the Middle Ages among the poor as well as the rich. Usury was still forbidden by canon law, but lenders did not lend for nothing, and there were all kinds of subtle devices for cloaking usurious transactions. Perhaps, for example, the lender would note down as lent more money than was actually paid over, so that when the debt was settled the man who had borrowed really paid more than he had originally received. Or a fictitious sale may have been arranged, whereby the lender would pretend to have sold something to the borrower and immediately to have bought it back again at a smaller price. In this way, the borrower would be bound in the future to pay back a sum to the lender larger than that which he had initially received. Usury was one of those sins which theologians had originally condemned on theological and philosophical principles. But it became necessary to society, and it took the casuistry of canon lawyers to get round the church's terrible fulminations. Practicality always works out in human societies, and it is probably always organized by the lawyers, who live in the real world, rather than by the theologians who, anyhow in the Middle Ages, tended only to inhabit eternity. Readers may be able to think of parallel examples at the present day.

Most obscure of all in later medieval England were the really poor and those, relatively few, who remained tied with the yoke of legal bondage. We know that villeins continued to exist into the sixteenth century here and there. At Forncett in Norfolk sixteen servile families remained in 1400, doing rough labour of building and repairing walls, though their servile work was less onerous than it once had been. They might take leases of land formerly free, but once in their hands it was referred to as 'soiled' land. By 1500 some eight bond families still resided, in 1525, five. Bond tenants during our period are to be found in many scattered localities. Sir Robert Bardolf of Oxfordshire left 3s. 4d. to be divided among his *nativi* (= 'bondmen') for losses in their grain.* There were bond servants in Richard II's London,† and the rebels of 1381 cried out that they wished to be free of all manner of *servage*, and that *nulle homme ne deveroit estre nayf.*‡ The problem of villeinage was a living one in Devonshire as late as 1437, when the Abbot of Tavistock was accused of releasing so many serfs from their bondage, especially women and girls, that the remaining villeins were deprived of women of their own condition with whom they could contract marriage.§ There will be more to say about these matters in the chapter which follows on class.

---

*Somerset House, will register 'Rous', folios 8 and 9. Evidence of villeinage in various counties in the fifteenth century can also be found in the *Calendar of Close Rolls*, published by the Stationery Office.

†Ranulf Higden, *Polychronicon* (ed. J. R. Lumby, Rolls Series), vol. IX (1886), p. 277.

‡*Anonimalle Chronicle*, edited by V. H. Galbraith, Manchester University Press, 1927, pp. 144—5.

§*The Register of Edmund Lacy, Bishop of Exeter 1420—55*, edited by G. R. Dunstan, Canterbury and York Society and Devon and Cornwall Record Society, Torquay, 1967, pp. 219—20.

4 Class

'I suppose you know that I am not accustomed to meddle with lords' matters much more than I need. . . .' The writer was John Paston,* and he knew well enough that England was politically still an aristocratic country in which it was dangerous for country gentlemen such as he to strike out a line of their own against the wishes of the country's masters.

For all that, fifteenth-century England was a land in which men felt a sharpening self-consciousness about their social status. In much the same way, Victorian England suffered an acute attack of snobbery through the efforts of that intensely mobile society to establish a comfortable sense of inner security. If in the late Middle Ages a stronger sense of identity in opposition to the world beyond the seas was creating an incipient nationalism, it is no less true that Englishmen were increasingly conscious of the status (here for colloquial convenience called class) which divided them from each other, precisely because the redistribution of wealth called for modes of behaviour to justify the *nouveau riche* to himself on the one hand, and to assert on the other the immemorial predominance of the lord. England was never a caste society, though some would have wished to make it so. Castes as opposed to classes are supported by specific legal or religious rules, age-long in their hierarchical arrangement, and made rigid by unbreakable conventions about marriage, inheritance and even places of dwelling, so that its members may quickly and without difficulty be identified by a glance at their physical appearance. In western Europe, society never quite attained so stiff an organization, despite the *parage* of the French nobility that made peers of *all* a nobleman's sons, and despite the classic but literary and soon-decayed division between those who fight, and those who pray, and those who labour. For one thing, the ethnic groups were too mixed; for another, the Christian religion by its very origins and nature rejected true social

Paston Letters, ɪ, No. 255.

exclusiveness. Christianity may have begun as a religion of the poor, but it was more deeply a religion of brotherhood in which there were neither bond nor free. It began by tolerating social divisions which seemed of little account in a world where the end of all things was at hand. If, during our period, it displayed a certain formalism under the control of the rich, it was none the less a religion shared by people of all classes, whose families divided and moved across economic and social frontiers, and whose priesthood was in many ways the only career open to talent alone. As the total wealth of Christendom increased in the early Middle Ages, and became redistributed in the later, a quicker social mobility becomes visible. The stresses of these movements created class-consciousness for the paradoxical reason that class frontiers were becoming for the time being increasingly blurred.

Even Frenchmen, who could sneer that the English had no peerage, were subject to these changes. They might live under the rule of *parage* instead of the English primogeniture which kept, in feudal families, title and patrimony for the eldest son alone, leaving the others to fend for themselves and become absorbed into the ranks of commoners. But chance and the fragmentation of wealth brought enormous differences to the noble *lignages* of France. In Forez men of noble extraction might live a hand-to-mouth existence of penury, fail to make good marriages, and fall into the hands of money-lenders. Professor Perroy has calculated that the Forez nobility lost half of its members within any given century, and that the average duration of a noble line was three to four generations. There, as elsewhere, their ranks were replenished from royal servants of baser stock, lawyers, burgesses or even the peasantry. It was easy enough for a prosperous man to call himself noble after a while. Such men could always fabricate an ancestry if they wanted, for instance, to enter an exclusive religious institution like the Knights Hospitaller or the cathedral chapter of Lyon. People became *gentil* by acquiring fiefs, or marrying into *gentilesse*, thus making themselves acceptable to the existing gentry. In Provence, the splitting of fiefs among children without regard to age or sex in the eleventh and twelfth centuries meant that by the thirteenth century numbers of 'nobles' were living the same rough and simple lives as their peasants. They began, however, to understand the danger. Certain bold families began to take advantage of the Roman law that allowed testators to exclude daughters, and this exclusion had become quite customary by the fourteenth century. Jacques d'Agoult wrote in 1361: 'I will that as long as there is anyone in my family in the male line, no woman shall succeed to my inheritance.' This became universal and statutory in 1472, applying to all successions, whether noble or not, 'in the name of preservation for noble and other houses'. After the fifteenth century, the nobility of France was able for economic and other reasons to rebuild itself more as a privileged class, but the late medieval intermixture of noble and bourgeois continued, and the end of the Middle Ages has for that reason been styled an era of *paix sociale*. On a lower level, the rich serfs of the Nivernais in the 1440s were resisting seignorial rights over the marriage of their daughters and declaring that they would marry off their girls as they pleased, '*en noblesse et bourgeoisie*'.

By a strange reversal the English feudal classes were at the self-same time adjusting themselves to mobility from the opposite direction, as in the late fourteenth and the fifteenth centuries primogeniture's single-minded logic could be overcome by the device known as the 'enfeoffment to use'. By this means a man who held land in primogeniture could during his own life-time make it over by a written legal act to a group of trustees. These trustees then held the land in common-law estate, but in actuality to the 'use' of the original owner, so that during his lifetime he in fact lost nothing. Before his death such a man would execute a document called a 'last will' (*ultima voluntas*) in which he expressed his wishes for the distribution of this estate after his death. When he died, the royal or lord's official who might expect to seize the estate and exact feudal dues before passing it on to the single heir would find that the dead man had, according to the common law, left nothing that could be so handled. 'Long before his death,' their reports usually ran, 'he had deprived himself of his estate. . . .' By the fifteenth century this practice was spreading quite rapidly, and the Latin 'testaments' which bequeathed movable goods and chattels, and were mostly proved by the church courts, come more and more often to be followed by 'last wills', frequently written in French or English, and giving minute directions for the partition of real estate. In this way, the transference of land after the death of its holder became more flexible, and younger brothers and even daughters could have their needs catered for. Of course, the trustees, or 'feoffees to use', could be dishonest, and the common-law courts could offer no remedy to the survivors. But mostly they did their duty faithfully. They were, after all, well-known and generally respectable characters, and would be paid for their pains. By the fifteenth century, too, such arrangements could be protected by the court of Chancery which dispensed not common law but 'equity', or the rules of fair play and what contemporaries sometimes called 'natural justice'. Enfeoffments to use played their part in the changing class-structure of the country by allowing a more flexible and wider distribution of property, depriving king and feudal lords of some income and seignorial rights, and making the special character of feudal tenure less important.

The Court of Chancery in the fifteenth century: protector of petitioners who sought 'natural justice'.

Increasingly it mattered how much land you had: decreasingly it mattered in what tenure you held it.

In Germany too, the Middle Ages saw the elevation of court officials to noble status. In central Europe a sharpening of social oppositions through social mobility was experienced. This may be illustrated by an anti-Hussite tract written by Andrew of Ratisbon in the first half of the fifteenth century which contains the following dialogue between a priest and a peasant:

PEASANT: It seems good that we should not be oppressed by the lords.
PRIEST: How so?
PEASANT: It is certain that all should be equal.
PRIEST: If you like such a state of affairs, how would it please you if your servant came into your own house, where you are the lord, and wanted to be equal with you?

Plate 1. Building operations in the fifteenth century, shown in a French representation of the Tower of Babel

PEASANT: That would not do at all.
PRIEST: Why not?
PEASANT: That sort of thing wouldn't work [*Res ista stare non posset*].
PRIEST: Well, why not? What would you prefer?
PEASANT: It is better that due order be observed and, as in old custom, inferiors be subject to superiors.*

At this point it might be incidentally noted that in the later Middle Ages both English and European society were unripe for post-industrial political doctrines of secular revolutionism. Social protest there was, but it was mostly expressed in religious or quasi-religious terms. One is still in the margin between social and religious protest, as any student of Hus or Wyclif and the Lollards can see. Dr Hobsbawm, in his brilliant book on *Primitive Rebels*, points out that this passionate longing for a new order in the world was 'millenniarist' in character. It occurred in societies deeply affected by Judaic or Christian ideas, where it was easy to believe that a new age lay just round the corner if only people would see it. Men did not understand the economic preconditions of change. In eastern countries with religious traditions like Hinduism, however, it was difficult to construct even millenarian ideologies, for the world was thought of as in constant flux or in a series of cyclical movements, so that nothing was stable and true caste was more firmly established.

By the later Middle Ages, then, the original exclusive contrast in western European society between warring noble and cultivating peasant had been all but overcome. It was destroyed by economic progress, that is, the creation and then the redistribution of wealth, and the foundation of intermediate classes whose ambitions pressed ever upwards in imitation of supposedly aristocratic behaviour. In doing these things, such classes aspired to what they regarded as an aristocratic norm of *gentilesse* or gentility, not realizing, of course, that their actions were in reality creating something quite different, namely, a new 'gentility' itself, which connoted gentle behaviour in an actual sense, quite unlike the rough lives of a warrior nobility 'whose manners matched their finger nails'. This is why a chapter dealing with class in the late Middle Ages must be above all preoccupied with the concept of the gentleman.

It is not that the words *'generosus'*, *'gentil'* or 'gentleman', all roughly

*This dialogue is quoted in the original Latin in the journal *Annales*, Paris, 1961, p. 1060, note 5.

Plate 2. Spinning wool. An early fifteenth-century picture from France

equivalent, were wholly new. On the contrary, *'gentilhomme'* was in France already a current word for nobleman by the twelfth century. At the same time, Alexander Neckham, an English schoolman, applied the word *'generosus'* to knights, and spoke of gentleness of blood (*'sanguinis generositas'*). In 1204 a Somersetshire man, asking the sheriff to deal justly with his family, said that they were native born and local gentry — *'naturales homines et gentiles de patria'*. Bishop Grosseteste of Lincoln in the earlier thirteenth century (himself accused of servile birth) spoke of the priestly duty of preaching, and noted an argument used by some to excuse themselves this obligation on the grounds of their own importance: 'I cannot preach because I am a gentleman [*quia generosus sum*] — a great clerk, lecturing in arts or physic.' Yet at this earlier time 'gentle' meant 'noble' in distinction from base or peasant-like. True, it foreshadowed the usage or concept of the modern world in which a man was, until recently, either 'a gentleman' or not, irrespective of any title or wealth he might possess. But it did not really connote the subtler use of gentleman that appeared in fifteenth-century England to denote one who was neither noble nor base.

In England the harsh oppositions were already fading by the thirteenth century, as the urban population grew and the knightly classes, often unable to afford the equipment of war, were becoming ruralized, turning from armour and chargers to local government and the running of their own estates. The criterion of knighthood was changing from birth to wealth, but it was a difficult criterion to apply. Knights who owed their status to family tradition were becoming fewer. Attempts were made by the king's government to compel men worth about £20 a year to be made knights. This was known as 'distraint of knighthood'. Often such men simply did not wish to do this: it involved various obligations which were expensive or irksome. Sometimes local officials who should strictly speaking have been knights, 'girt with the sword', had to be replaced by others who, though well-to-do and therefore respectable, were not knights in name. Yet men did join the ranks of knighthood, often through career success in the royal service. Our snobbish friend Froissart noted of Sir Robert Salle, governor of Norwich in 1381, that he had been knighted by King Edward for his ability and courage, *though he was not of gentle birth.* *

The same interpenetration of classes occurred at all levels. The late fourteenth and the fifteenth centuries in England formed an age of ambition, of upward class movements. The nobility were criticized and infiltrated by

---

Chronicles, Book II, Chapter 76.

the knightly commons; the gentry were both crystallizing as a class yet being attacked and infiltrated from below; the upper bourgeoisie was assimilating itself to the gentry through intermarriage and the acquisition of possessions. Below this again, the lesser bourgeoisie of shopkeepers and skilled artisans were proliferating and often showing intense hostility to those above them in the social scale.

Naturally enough, the old upper classes felt themselves threatened, and strove with the impotent weapons of legislation or ridicule to maintain their status.

From 1363 onwards there was a continuous stream of parliamentary acts for the 'reformation of excessive array', which have been diversely inter-preted as a wish to protect home industries by discouraging the import of foreign luxuries, and as an attempt to curb the extravagant fashion-consciousness of both clergy and pious Christian laity. Though there is force behind both these economic and moral motives, the social fear felt by men of estate for their ebullient inferiors was none the less strongly expressed in them. The statute of 1363 certainly referred directly to the 'outrageous and excessive apparel of divers people against their estate and degree', and the acute canon of Leicester put into words a widespread feeling when in 1388 he wrote of

the elation of the inferior people in dress and accoutrements in these days, so that one person cannot be discerned from another in splendour of dress or belongings, neither poor from rich, nor servant from master, nor priest from layman; but every-body tried to imitate the other, till the magnates had to decide on a remedy.*

Even in 1361, to take another small but curious example, a finder of a stray hawk might only keep it, if the owner could not be found, 'sil soit gentil homme'; otherwise it was to go to the sheriff.

The new nobility themselves did not escape the censures of snobbery. The De la Poles, merchants of Hull, financiers and lenders to the king, who rose to be Earls and then Dukes of Suffolk, were perhaps the most remarkable contemporary examples of social climbing, and ended so near the throne that Henry VIII thought it prudent to remove the head of John de la Pole. But men of the later Middle Ages were quite aware of such origins. Thomas Walsingham, with the flair for social discernment not uncommon in Benedictine monks, wrote in 1385 of the Earl of Suffolk as 'a man more suitable for trade than knighthood, as he had spent his life as a money

*Knighton's Chronicon, II, p. 299.

merchant, not a soldier'.* In 1465 it was still possible for John Paston to write

... as for the pedigree of the said Duke [of Suffolk], he is son to William Pool, Duke of Suffolk, son to Michael Pool, Earl of Suffolk, son to Michael Pool, the first Earl of Suffolk of the Pools ... and the said first Michael was son to one William Pool of Hull, which was a worshipful man grown to fortune of the world. ... †

In 1460 Lord Rivers was rated by three earls at Calais who pointed out that they were of the king's blood and he only a squire's son, and made by marriage. Politics apart, they had little enough reason for such vanity. Professor Lander has not only defended the Rivers family convincingly against the accusations that they were upstarts, but has written of England in general much the same analysis of the aristocracy as Professor Perroy made of Forez:

The idea of the 'old nobility' has been very much overworked. Baronial families seem to have died out in the male line about every third generation. Of the noble families in existence in 1485, half had been extinguished in the male line by 1547, and there is no reason to believe that the proportion was less in the mid fifteenth century. This high mortality meant that the honours of a large section of the nobility do not go very far back. Between 1439 and 1504 there were 68 new creations of peers. Of these, only 21 were for the husbands or sons of old peerage heiresses, leaving 47 completely new creations. The nobility had to be constantly recruited from below, and its basis was plutocratic rather than aristocratic.

The same mobility occurred all down the scale. To Froissart, as to other chroniclers, the shocking revolt of 1381 could be attributed to 'the ease and riches that the common people are of'. If the rebels of 1381 shouted that they wanted to be free of all kinds of servitude and loathed the pretensions of the gentry, so too the more literate and cultivated classes never ceased to look upon their social inferiors as dangerous in act and beastly in appearance. Adam of Usk commented on the beheading in 1400 of Lord Despenser by workmen at Bristol:

... seeing that all these things were done only by the savage fury of the people, I fear that they will make this a plea to wield still more in future against their lords the power of the sword, which has now been allowed to them, against all system of order.

*Thomas Walsingham, *Historia Anglicana* (edited by H. T. Riley, Rolls Series, 1863), II, 141; cf. 146.
†*Paston Letters*, II, No. 514.

A gentleman dresses in comfort by the fire, *c.* 1320.

Richard II's Cheshire archers were to the same writer

by nature bestial, not drawn from the gentlemen of the countryside but from rustics or tailors or artisans.... Men who at home were hardly worthy to take off the shoes of their masters have behaved like the equals and fellows of lords.*

Among the gentry a sense of danger bred a sense of fellow feeling for each other which has perhaps never quite ceased to endure. In 1455 when the faithful Devonshire lawyer, Nicholas Radford, was woken in the night by the gang that was to murder him, he came to his window and called out into the confusion of voices and waving lights to ask if there were a gentleman among them with whom he might speak. Sir Thomas Courtenay, a perjured ruffian, then promised on the fealty by which he was bound to God and 'as I am a gentleman and a faithful knight' that Radford would suffer no harm.

Much later, in Henry VIII's time, one of the Plumptons wrote to protest to a neighbour about quite a minor matter, asking him to let one of his own tenants have a previous right of way, and crowning his letter with the plea 'that he may gentle have the same, as one gentleman and gentlewoman may use one another with favour'.†

The idea that society in western Europe was fundamentally divided between the *gentilhomme* and the rest was much older than the fifteenth century and overrode other hierarchical distinctions. Yet about 1420 in England the description of men by their class or status began to evolve much more

*Adam of Usk, *Chronicon* (edited and translated by E. M. Thompson, 1904), pp. 43, 203.
†*Plumpton Correspondence*, p. 245.

rapidly. This was partly the result of the quicker social mobility which has been described, partly of the increasing use of the English language in official documents, and partly an almost accidental result, in an age of increasing litigation amongst people of middling degree, of the Statute of Additions (1413) which insisted that in certain legal actions the defendant must be described with extreme accuracy if the action were not to fail through mis-description and faulty use of words. This sometimes resulted in over-elaborate descriptions of men. For example, to call John Thame of Fairford, junior, husband alias merchant alias gentleman alias woolman alias yeoman, was not only to comment obliquely upon a real ambiguity, but to pepper the legal target with shots in order to make certain that at least one of them hit the bull's-eye. This is not quite equivalent to saying that England was becoming a more class-ridden society, but it pointed to a continual in-trospective distinction men were making about themselves and each other. Status, after all, is not an objective thing but depends upon what *other* people think of you. In the fifteenth century many people wished to be accounted gentlemen, or to marry them, many people thought they were gentlemen, or wished they were, or made similar decisions about others, and many people entered the ranks of the gentry from below. Again, this was not exactly related to income, as we all know. There is a time-lag in these matters, otherwise the concepts of *nouveau riche* and decayed gentlefolk could not exist. Did not someone say, to take a modern instance, that the public schools of Britain were for the fathers of gentlemen, not their sons? But Geoffrey Chaucer in his time recognized as well as any modern sociologist that 'gentility' was ultimately the consequence of enrichment:

> But for ye speken of swich gentilesse
> As is descended out of old richesse
> That therefore sholden ye be gentil men,
> Swich arrogance is nat worth an hen.*

More precisely, the recognition of gentle status in later medieval England depended upon both having and being certain things.

To be meant to have. Every estate or rank, if it were not to be lost, was marked by certain possessions or 'gear'. In 1461 the future Sir John Paston received a letter saying

And John Jeney informed me ... you are inbilled to be made knight at this coronation. Whether you have understood beforehand I know not but, if it please

The Wife of Bath's Tale, lines 1109—11.

you to take the worship upon you considering the comfortable tidings aforesaid, and for the gladness and pleasure of all your well-wishers and to the pain and discomfort of your ill-willers, it were time your gear necessary on that behalf were purveyed for, and also you have need to hie you to London for, as I conceive, the knights should be made upon the Saturday before the coronation.*

The same mentality was at work when parliament in 1429 confined the election of parliamentary knights in the county courts to those people who had freehold property worth at least 40s. a year and in doing so noted a distinction between people worth this amount, whom it called '*les gentils*', and the others:

> Because elections of the knights of the shires to come to the king's parliaments . . . have recently been made by too great and excessive numbers of people in the counties, of whom the large part are people of small possessions or of no value, who each pretend to have an equivalent vote in such elections to the most worthy knights or esquires in the counties, whereby homicides, riots, batteries and divisions are likely to arise *entre les gentils et autres gentz* . . . [therefore the knights are to be elected by residents of the counties who have free tenements to the value of at least 40s. per annum net.]†

John Paston certainly was thinking along these lines in 1461 when he wrote that it would be for the quiet of the country and more 'worshipful' if a record were made 'of all such as might spend 40s. a year' on the day of the election.‡

The criterion of possessions was sometimes taken to lengths which seem absurd. A testator in 1415 left to his son a good deal of household linen which included 'a paire of newe gentilmenshetis . . . and a pair of yeoman's sheets'.§ Yeomen bought and sold land and were sometimes in fact richer than acknowledged gentry. But they were not supposed to be. In 1475 Sir William Plumpton was told of a new rule made in Chancery that no sureties should be accepted 'but such as be sufficient . . . so it is hard to get sureties for a yeoman'.‖ One Stonor correspondent referring to a landed title-deed called it '. . . a gentlymanly thynge, a copy of the Kynges Recordes'.¶

---

*Paston Letters, II, No. 391.
†Statutes of the Realm, II, pp. 243–4. On the 40 shilling 'barrier', see also p. 15 above.
‡Paston Letters, II, No. 402.
§Register of Archbishop Chichele, edited by E. F. Jacob (Oxford 1938), II, 46, 48.
‖Plumpton Correspondence, 29–30.
¶Stonor Letters, No. 65.

Many of these texts which define a gentleman in the fifteenth century are legal ones. To be taken for a gentleman was often expressed in this way, largely because legal texts are hard evidence and perpetuate for us, by their very survival, the ways in which people thought. But the legal profession itself was one of the main highroads to gentle estate. Naturally, there were far fewer professions then than there are now, but then as now a successful professional career could set the seal upon a man's social advancement. Such were the Church, Medicine (about which we know little) and, above all, the Law. A career in law was one of the few ways to accumulate great wealth, and the common lawyers played an important part in founding new gentry families, and in supporting with large dowries and jointures the more ancient ones. Families like the Brudenells, Townsends and Dudleys originated thus. The Pastons sent boys to the Inns of Court in London to become apprentices in the law, not only to learn skills in defending or augmenting the family fortune, but to become qualified and to cut a figure. A really successful man there would sooner or later take the great step of becoming a 'serjeant-at-law' and then joining the Bench of his Inn. From the ranks of Benchers were drawn the Barons of the Exchequer, law officers of the Crown, and Recorders of many of the larger towns. It was not unlike the promotion of a modern physician or surgeon to be a consultant in a hospital, if we substitute Inn of Court for London Teaching Hospital (and perhaps compare the medieval anxiety about suitable surnames, which will be discussed in a minute, with the rash of freshly hyphenated names to be found on brass plates in Harley street). The Inns of Court were equivalent to the University for Common Lawyers, since at Oxford and Cambridge only Roman civil law and the canon law were taught, apart, of course, from the arts, medicine and theology.

Oxford and Cambridge remained the preserve of the clergy, and to go thither certainly helped on clerical careers, but these, though they might lead to high status, were of an entirely different quality and were, by reason of the rule of celibacy, of little or no importance in the foundation of gentry families. The new layman and would-be government servant who looked forward to marriage turned rather to the Inns, scattered about the environs of Chancery Lane. Many came, but many dropped out of the professional career. The serjeant-at-law was lucky. He passed through a bottleneck, for the vacancies were few. But when and if he succeeded he joined the Order of the Coif and wore as his badge of distinction a white head-dress which is the ancestor of the legal wig. If a serjeant lived long enough he was almost certain to become a royal judge. Then, as now, legal promotion might mean some loss of income through private practice, but the compensation for a monopoly of pleading in the High Courts was an assured income through salary and expenses on circuit. Judges of the central courts were, for example, paid at a standard rate of 20s. a day when they were on circuit as commissioners of Oyer and Terminer, and this included the time of 'their going, abiding and coming homeward', and they got their money with a speed remarkable in that age of dilatory and uncertain remuneration. The days on which they actually worked in court might be few in relation to those spent journeying or hanging about while cases were prepared, but they were paid for the whole time.*

Their wills show their wealth. Justice Vavasour who was a serjeant left money and plate in six separate repositories, including £800 in gold in Axholme Priory. Many bought land and collected books. Lawyers, like other materially successful members of society, attracted their full share of dislike, and one parliament even tried to exclude lawyers from the ranks of M.P.s on the ground that they were only there to further their clients' interests. Lawyers were also a particular target for the rebels of 1381, since they were associated, as lawyers always are, with the dominance of property and the existing régime. But of course the lawyers triumphed socially and became an integral part of the new gentry from then onwards.

Just as to be meant to have, so having affected being. It is no surprise that to be a gentleman in the fifteenth century connoted a code of external behaviour and manners. It was not just a matter of having a private seal for one's letters, bearing some family badge or device. Every Tom, Dick and Harry was having these made, and until the Heraldic Visitations under the Tudors the assumption of badges or coats of arms was relatively uncontrolled. Nicholas Upton, writing in the fifteenth century, debated whether arms given by princes were of greater or less dignity than arms assumed on a man's own authority, and commented acidly, 'in these days we openly see how many poor men, labouring in the French wars, are become noble . . . of whom many of their own authority have assumed arms to be borne by themselves and their heirs'. What counted was how you were called and how you behaved. Even names mattered. It was much better to have a name derived from a place than from a trade or a nickname. In 1487 a bachelor was admitted at Merton College, Oxford, called 'Hugh Sawnder otherwise known as

*Judith B. Avrutick, 'Commissions of Oyer and Terminer in Fifteenth-century England' (Unpublished London M. Phil. thesis, 1967), 63. I am grateful to my former pupil, Miss Avrutick, for permission to use this reference.

Shakespere, but his name has been changed because the old one was not well thought of (*quia vile reputatum est*)'.*

Every fifteenth-century book of 'nurture', or etiquette – and there were more and more of them – was about the external behaviour expected of the 'gentle'. *'Gentilesse'* ought to be interpreted literally. It made much of quietness and restraint in speech: to be *gentil of langage*. Such a one rises from table quietly, thanks his host and

> Alle the gentyllys togydre yn-same ...
> Than men wylle say therafter
> That a gentylleman was heere....

The converse was the acknowledged boorishness of the non-gentry, and this became a literary convention. Sir Edmund Chambers, writing on the *Morte D'Arthur*, said 'the distinction between noble and churl was fundamental. If there are sparks of nobility in a cowherd's son or a kitchen knave, you may be sure he will turn out to be a king's son in disguise.' This went along with a contempt for manual labour. Craftsmen who throve and became entrepreneurs had to remove all traces of their old trade from their lives if they wished to be accepted as members of the livery company or society bearing the name of the trade from which their prosperity was originally derived. A working dyer was merely a 'bluenails'. Commerce was less disgraceful as a craft. The well-to-do Leicestershire family of Randolff accumulated land between 1200 and 1500 at Wigston and became 'gentlemen', yet Richard Randolff, gentleman, did not disdain to become Richard Randolff, grocer, of Leicester. Prosperity was the main thing. If you were 'gentle born', so much the better; if you were a financier or a merchant, that was all right, though you might meet with rebuffs; if you were an artisan or a labourer, you belonged to a different world. In 1383 supercilious Thomas Walsingham obliquely pointed to the social rise of merchants when he referred to the military uselessness of certain French soldiers in the Low Countries who were not like the gallant knights of old but 'delicate youths, sons of merchants and burgesses, knowing nothing of arms'.† There were other writers in fifteenth-century England who regretted the passing of true knighthood and alluded contemptuously to the modern gentleman's preoccupation with estate management and productive self-enrichment.

Registrum Annalium collegii Mertonensis, 1483–1521, edited by H. E. Salter (Oxford Hist. Soc. LXXVI, 1923), 98.
†*Historia Anglicana*, II, p. 104.

So far no attention has been paid to the problem of accent as a sign of class speech, so evident in later days and (we are always being told) peculiar to the class-ridden society of England. In fact, a 'class accent' was in England a very much later development. It is quite true that later medieval men tried hard to change their behaviour, or at least that of their children, to make them acceptable in 'superior' company. Chaucer's Franklin could not stop talking about his ambitions for his son and his disappointment that the boy, who had plenty of money, would not mix in the right company:

> And he had lever talken with a page
> Than to commune with any gentil wight
> Ther he mighte lerné gentilesse aright. . . .

until he is snubbed for his snobbery —

> Straw for your gentilessé, quod our hoste. . . .

But in the later Middle Ages, class accent, if not entirely non-existent, was certainly very underdeveloped. One has only to recall that in the early seventeenth century Sir Walter Raleigh, that epitome of the fashionable man, spoke with a strong Devonshire accent. In the fifteenth century, differences in speech were regional rather than social. A successful draper of, say, Coventry, would talk in a manner much less different from his Coventry craftsmen than a modern business executive from his work-people on the shop floor. A rich man might have his children taught French. Trevisa himself noted that 'uplandish' men tried to learn French to liken themselves to gentlemen. But they would not pick up a different English accent. One may guess that the importance of pronunciation as a measure of status was just beginning to assert itself here and there. It has already been seen that royal justices and messengers from the central administration carried southern speech modes into the extremities of the kingdom. There is also Master John Chalurys of Bridport, who lived about 1400 and is credited with the composition of a treatise on speech; at the end of it a note is added, saying that his book offers an improved method of pronunciation whereby readers can be called more noble (*'per quos lectores dicantur nobiliores'*).* But it is dubious how much effect this had. Probably the earliest differentiation between polite and vulgar English speech lay not in pronunciation but in choice of words and avoidance of dialect. When Skelton and Ben Jonson wanted to hold the uneducated up to ridicule, they made them speak not Cockney or any other special pronunciation but the

*Dean and Chapter of Lincoln MS. 88, fo. 129v.

vernacular dialect of some outlying province, especially the south-west, or else distort hard words like skeleton or dudgeon into ludicrous forms like 'skellington' and 'dungeon'. In fact, the first writer who ridiculed vulgar London pronunciation was, it seems, James Elphinston, whose derided Cockney character was actually a courtier. The crucial time for this important change was the middle of the eighteenth century. At that period numerous pronouncing dictionaries began to appear: Johnson's in 1764, Elphinston's in 1765, and so on. The self-assertion of newly enriched industrial classes now obeyed not the aristocrat but the pedagogue. Elphinston said the best English was spoken in the metropolis, not at the court. Lord Chesterfield himself wrote

> The common people of every country speak their own language very ill; the people of fashion, as they are called, speak it better, but not always correctly, because they are not always people of letters. Those who speak their own language the most accurately are those who have learning and are at the same time in the polite world; at least, their language will be reckoned the standard one of that country.

All the time, the children of poorer classes in social isolation adhered to the older, looser system, while their language was also more exposed to sound changes and innovations. Cockney shows a retention of old-fashioned and dialect forms together with new and 'advanced' forms, like turning vowels into diphthongs or simply changing them: 'loike' for 'like', 'nime' for 'name', 'nar' for 'now'. Perhaps a vital role in social speech-changes, and, indeed, most forms of external manners, lies with women, with their keener sense of imitation and their swifter adaptability to surroundings, as well as with their nurture of the very young.

It would be the profoundest mistake in writing of a new age of ambition and *gentilesse* to behave like so many historians in ignoring the feminine role. The softening of real manners owed much to them, as any reader of the books of etiquette can see, or, for the matter of that, anyone who reflects for a single moment about present-day life. Perhaps the Paston women spelled 'worse' than their menfolk, in the sense that their orthography was often more unusual and even contorted. But they, as always, must have been active in the earliest lessons of their children. Their not infrequent literacy and the parts they were called upon to play in mercantile or affluent country families placed them in command of households which were now less war-like, less brutal (despite the well-advertised violence of the time) than the real aristocratic households of an earlier time, when women's work was narrower in scope, and when widows and dependants suffered more pitifully from the failures and forfeitures of their men.

It is much easier to write about aristocrats and gentlemen in the later Middle Ages than about class-feeling among the poorer groups of the population. Something has already been said of the attitude *towards* them, especially during the Great Revolt of 1381, or when they were in arms, supporting an unpopular ruler. But to find out how the poor themselves felt we have to search many kinds of literature, for they left few other memorials of their hearts and minds. Political poems and slogans, handed down obscurely, tell us they hated the gentry, rich clergy and lawyers. They enjoyed cutting off gentle heads in 1381. They hated labour services, less for their arduous nature than for their servile significance. They felt the stigma of bondage. 'Are we not all descended from the same parents?' Even in the thirteenth century there was a case, found by Professor Hilton, where a man drowned himself rather than suffer the name of villein. Sermon literature in English, explored by Dr Owst,* gives expression to 'the woes of a voiceless multitude of common men and women suffering from daily wrongs and injustices of all kinds', and the growth of English literature in pulpit or manuscript carries with it a solemn indignation, pessimism and bitterness. Probably the original authors of this bitter stuff were the minor clergy themselves, for the clergy were never a class but were distributed throughout all classes, distinguished from others only by their relatively greater literacy and therefore their enduring articulateness. From mysterious wandering preachers sprang satire against officials, against the pride of the rich, and against church courts where the poor man was hammered harder than the gentleman who could the more easily commute his penances for money. This is why the great and angelic *Vision of Piers the Plowman* is not wholly original but rests on a vast, scarcely known collection of mutterings:

> . . . lewed men ne coude
> Iangle ne iugge, that iustifie hem shulde;
> But suffren and serven.†

In the thirteenth century the mendicant friars, or some of them, were champions of the poor, but by the late fourteenth century the mendicant art of protest had passed to wilder men who would use these weapons of satire against the very Orders that fashioned them. Some of these protesters were

*G. R. Owst, *Literature and Pulpit in Medieval England*, second edition, 1961, especially pp. 215—23.
†Text B, Prologue, lines 129—31.

Left A Kentish peasant in 1390, forced to perform carrying service. *Right* Friars depicted with a devil on their backs. Many people thought the friars had betrayed the poor.

Lollards. There was, for example, an outbreak of Lollardy in Exeter in 1421, when the Franciscan chapel there was desecrated and glass windows portraying the arms of Henry V were smashed. The motive was hostility against the burial privileges of the rich. There is also a poem against the rich written about the same time in Latin Goliardic metre, of which a rough modern translation may be hazarded here:

These little friars preachify, and swear, as they will have it,
If a fellow pass away in the Minors' habit,
Of such a soul it can be said the Devil shall not grab it,
But instantly the angels shall to heavenly mansions drag it.
So thus a rich man in the town, when taken very poorly,
Will find a friar hurrying and worrying so sorely
That he should be in time to see the patient pass to glory,
But not before he's left his corpse to the friar's church most surely.
Yet if a pauper at his death is heard for friars calling
To ask a final resting-place where friars' prayers are falling,
'The Warden, sad to say, is out', says any friar, stalling,
And thus the poor man shuts his eyes to snubs he'd reckon galling.*

Our age was one of ambition and upward striving, though class mobility had its casualties in those who fell or who were left behind. The friction was harsh in a time of amelioration, even if some rich people loved their servants and cared for them. Wealth, so conspicuous, became eagerly sought by more people. But new possibilities beget new tensions. Covetousness becomes a prominent sin. Lady Meed becomes a literary figure, and her bounty has a very bitter taste.

*R. Foreville, 'Manifestations de Lollardisme à Exeter en 1421.' *Le Moyen Age,* LXIX (1963), pp. 691–706, where the Latin original is printed.

A friar hears a confession. Their penances were said to be light.

5 Marriage and Sex

(a) The theory of marriage

To understand this subject it is necessary to go back a long way before 1350. Ideas about the relationship between men and women changed much less in western Christendom during the Middle Ages or, for that matter, during the early modern centuries, than did any of the other developments discussed in this book. For this reason it may be useful to explain what churchmen thought marriage was in order thus to sketch in a background to the thoughts and behaviour of later medieval men and women in general. This explanation in its turn may form a useful introduction to the social study of more modern times.

That marriage should be monogamous, of one man to one woman (*'unius ad unam'*), has endured, centuries long, as a basic Judaeo-Christian assumption up until the present day. Despite this, the ideas that lay behind this insistence, the reasons for it and the exceptions made to it, have shifted from time to time. Likewise, the essential nature of the marriage contract has changed somewhat. And it need hardly be said that monogamy does not, and did not, necessarily mean that a man or a woman could contract only one marriage in the lifetime of each, since remarriage on the death of one partner was always a possibility, while the whole apparatus of impediments and nullity rulings, quite apart from illicit relationships, frequently meant that even in the lifetime of a couple, one or both of them might experience more than one union which – to all intents and purposes at the time – was an acknowledged marriage. Monogamy, therefore, must be understood as at most a theoretical ideal, not in physical fact an irrefragable code of behaviour.

In the earlier Middle Ages a looser discipline which allowed divorce and remarriage prevailed among the Germanic peoples, although the Church's strict teaching against divorce in the modern sense was upheld. Roman law and some barbarian codes allowed divorce by mutual consent. Theologians

Plate 3. An Italian banking and counting house of the fourteenth century. The Italians were leaders in financial techniques

and canonists were busily at work, but the papacy did not always speak with an unambiguous voice. The 'reform of the Church' in the eleventh century, however, tightened up the whole issue, and the Church's intransigeance became total. True enough, the 'Pauline privilege', which permitted the re-marriage of a wedded convert if the pagan partner departed, was granted, but popes took a high view of even non-Christian matrimony. Above all, marriage came at that time to be regarded as a sacrament, precisely because the clerical reformers held that spiritual and rational things were 'higher' than physical ones. Just as the pope argued that he was superior to the emperor and the clergy superior to the layfolk, so the nature of matrimony was 'spiritualized' from the basically carnal to the basically spiritual, and a marriage grew to be regarded not as a relationship formed fundamentally by sexual union but by words spoken rationally. This rather oversimplified explanation is not intended to be taken as an approving or a disapproving one. It is what happened.

Such changes took place in a Christian world the past history of which had witnessed the deepest suspicion and even horror of sex and which was now, for better and for worse, affirming the pre-eminence of the rational, even though this new emphasis assuredly does not fit the facts of human sexuality altogether. The emotional attitude of Christian thinkers minimized the importance of coitus, and certain respected writers were deeply nervous about the rightness of pleasure itself. After all, as some argued, sexual orgasm momentarily overcomes rational thought in a manner not unlike drunkenness, and the sin of drunkenness has always been held to lie in the willing abandonment of the rational faculties. Even a Dominican friar and a great theologian, St Albert the Great, in the thirteenth century, held that carnal pleasure, though a certain good in itself, temporarily oc-cluded the sight of the prime Good. Probably the early patristic loathing of sex was by the thirteenth century being caught up in the new study of Aristotle, a philosopher now everywhere studied and revered, and for whom rationalism and calm contemplation were the best things in human life. For Aquinas, coitus for its own sake, even within marriage, had the tincture of sin about it. The disciplinary decrees which imposed celibacy on the clergy were enacted for various reasons, some of which had to do with an attempt to form a corps of clergy which could be appointed on its merits rather than as heirs of their fathers' benefices. But behind this again lay like a shadow the notion of bodily 'purity' among men who handled the sacred vessels and the Body of the Lord. Even the normal, involuntary emission of seminal fluid during sleep attracted to itself the name of 'nocturnal *pollution*', and there

Plate 4. Chaucer reading to a noble audience   81

Carving of a 'scolding wife' in Henry VII's chapel, Westminster Abbey. This was a favourite medieval motif among a celibate clergy who liked to remind people of matrimony's unattractive sides.

has lasted till this day in Roman Catholic manuals of pastoral theology the idea that sins of the flesh are in some way to be measured, or at least aggravated, by the very pleasure derived from them.

The twelfth century was a formative period in canon law, and in particular in the law of marriage. At that time the western Church was divided between two rival theories of the marriage bond. In the simplest terms, one view was that a marriage was only completed by its physical consummation. The consent of the two parties certainly began the marriage, but it was not entire and ratified until sexual intercourse had taken place. Indeed, this opinion must have reflected what has often really happened in village and town where the girl marries when she is pregnant by the man to whom she is engaged and who has already said or implied that he will marry her in the future. The betrothal, the promise relating to the future, played in any case a much more important part all through the Middle Ages than the engagement does today, and many people held that it became a real, valid marriage if it were followed by consummation, which often can only be proved by pregnancy. On the other hand, there was a powerful school of French ecclesiastics who held that the essence of the marriage bond was in the *words* the partners uttered to each other: 'I take thee for mine.' If these words were spoken in the present tense, then the marriage was made. This doctrine was in some ways a more sophisticated, more rational, more Roman one. It is effectively described in a rhymed instruction for parish priests in the fifteenth century:

> Here I take thee to my wedded wyf,
> And there-to I plyghte thee my trowthe
> Wyth-owten cowpulle or fleschly dede. . . .

It was a simple intellectual agreement, the *nudum pactum* of Roman law, effective even without witnesses, though witnesses had to be present to make it public and provable and therefore 'regular'. Pope Alexander III (1159–81), one of the greatest canonists, changed his mind about this matter. At first, he had held what may be called the 'consummation' view, but after he became pope he inclined to the consensual view, and ultimately this triumphed in the Roman Church. But for quite a long time it was held that a marriage could be formed *either* by a promise to marry in the future followed by physical consummation *or* by a promise to marry in the present. The ambiguity may be glimpsed in action, as it were, through a rule issued by the Bishop of Salisbury about 1219 which forbade a man 'to encircle the hands of a young woman with a ring of rush or other material, whether base or precious, in order the more easily to have his will of her, lest while he thinks he is joking he binds himself with the burdens of marriage'.*

We must remember therefore that however large a part was played in the making of medieval marriage by the kinsmen, the consent of the partners was absolutely necessary to make it valid in the eyes of the Church's law, and if one of the parties could prove the marriage had been forced by threats or contrived by deceptions, then it followed that a church court could pronounce it null from the beginning. It is also true that a decree of nullity could be obtained, as it still can, after a marriage 'by words in the present' if the marriage was not consummated; but in such a case the unwillingness or incapacity of one of the parties may be held to have affected the validity of the essential words spoken previously, and does not alter the basic distinction between the two different theories of marriage.

Needless to say, nullity proceedings could be dishonestly arranged, but there is no doubt that there were comparatively more frequent, genuine, proceedings of this kind than there are today, since the social structure

*_Councils and Synods_, edited by F. M. Powicke and C. R. Cheney, vol. ii, p. 87. The canon is mistranslated and misunderstood by G. C. Homans, _English Villagers in the Thirteenth Century_, p. 167.

allowed so much more family pressure upon marriageable people. Conversely, ecclesiastical law protected betrothals and marriages formed willingly by the partners against the wishes of their families, as the Pastons found to their cost in the famous case where a daughter decided to marry their bailiff. In 1469 the Bishop of Norwich did all he could to dissuade Margery and get her to change her mind, reminding her 'how she was born, what kin and friends she had and should have', but all was in vain, for she was defiant and regarded herself as *in conscience* bound to her Richard Calle. Failing to find any loophole that would nullify the betrothal, the bishop admitted that he could not pronounce a *divortium*.*

Alongside this doctrine of marriage there grew up a whole series of dispensations and impediments. For example, a girl forced into verbal consent could escape an unbearable marriage if before consummation she chose to retire into conventual life. Consent itself was ever more closely defined. It had to be lucid (the partner had to be sane); it had to be free from error (the partner had, for instance, to know if the intended spouse was of servile status); it had to be free from fear, which was and is hard enough to prove, and was held to be effectively disproved if coitus took place. Yet consent might be conveyed by proxies, or by signs instead of words. In 1402, King Henry IV was betrothed by proxy to Joan, Duchess of Brittany. At the ceremony the duchess was represented by her envoy, Antoine Ricze, who had brought a letter from her. The king placed a ring on the finger of the envoy, who, speaking for Joan, took Henry for the lady's husband. The actual marriage was performed the next year at Winchester with both parties present.

In an age when marriages were so often made in order to increase the worldly possessions of one or both of the partners, it was a nice question whether the doctrine that marriage was a sacrament conferring grace did not make marriages simoniacal, that is to say, equivalent to a purchase of sacramental grace. This matter was a difficult one for the scholastics to solve, but the Council of Florence in 1439 finally decided that sanctifying grace was certainly bestowed in matrimony through the reciprocal consent of the partners.† The true reasons for such consent in any particular case were not discussed.

Impediments were circumstances which made marriage either totally impossible in the eyes of the Church (*diriment impediments*) or else impossible without dispensation by ecclesiastical authority. The diriment impediments

---

Paston Letters, II, No. 617.

†H. Denziger, *Enchiridion Symbolorum* (edition of 1948), p. 259.

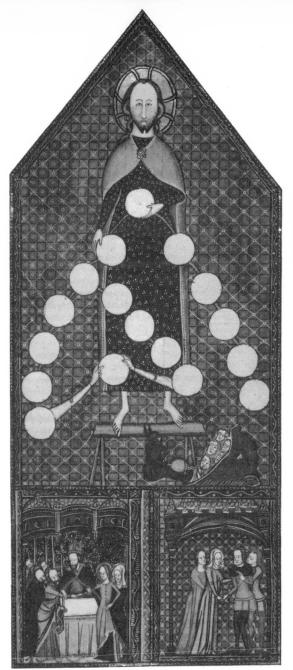

Left A diagram of consanguinity. 'Enquire how near they be of kindred, and whether they may marry together or not...' (*Paston Letters*, I, No. 225). *Above* The wedding ring. 'With this ring I thee wed, with my body and goods I thee honour.'

were fairly obvious: you could not marry someone bound by the priestly vow of celibacy, or someone with a valid spouse still living. Other impediments were less clear-cut. You could not marry a kinsman or kinswoman within a certain degree of relationship. After 1215 this was fixed at the fourth degree, though first cousins might on occasion be dispensed. This prohibition might mean that intending partners had to do some research. 'I pray you, cousin,' wrote Sir John Paston, 'enquire of my lady Felbridge how near they be of kindred, and whether they may marry together or not, and how many degrees in lineage they be asunder, for I report me to your wise discretion what the law will say therein.' * Dispensable impediments often had to do with 'affinity'. When two people got married, each acquired what was called an affinity with the kinsfolk of the other partner, and it was not possible to marry one of your affinity if your spouse died unless due permission were obtained. The original intention may have been to prevent domestic discord, though it is doubtful if such practical questions were the only reason. Impediments also came into existence against marriage with any relatives of a partner with whom the other partner had had illicit intercourse. Readers will remember that difficulties were created about the validity of Henry VIII's marriage with Anne Boleyn on the grounds of a previous affair with her sister Mary. Some even more far-fetched impediments were thought up by the severer theorists, though they were impossible to enforce. You could not marry your godparent. This first appears in the legislation of the Emperor Justinian (527–65), and derived from the notion that sponsorship at Christian initiation set up a metaphysical, other-worldly relationship which was held to be 'higher' even than natural parenthood. Here was another expression of comparative contempt for physical sexuality. This is why the parents could not be godparents to their own children: the sinful associations of venereal pleasure disqualified them from the godly privilege of assuming responsibility for the children. Some wilder writers even thought that subsequent copulation between godparents who were married to each other might be held incestuous. However this may be, such impediments multiplied as they became associated with confirmation as well as baptism.

The whole atmosphere was one of extreme legalism. We do not hear much of the pastoral side of the matter, though to be fair Aquinas wrote that the 'natural law' prescribed the immutability of wedlock for the good of the family and of society, and that a divorced wife would find herself at a disadvantage in getting another husband, and that anyhow she needed a man for

*Paston Letters, I, No. 225.

Left Lovers' meeting. The picture, like literary romantic love, originates in France.
Right The portrait by Holbein said to be of John Colet, Dean of St Paul's.

governance and friendship. But he thought that the personal factors of wedlock were outside the realm of legitimate theological study, and was content to be existentially ignorant of them.

Romantic love was, of course, outside the pale of the theological mind and entered only through the gates of southern French literature, more than a little tainted with heresy. It is remarkable how little is heard about children. The indissolubility of medieval wedlock was firmly based upon its sacramental character. Christ was thought of as wedded to His Church, and a bishop to his diocese. Today, the 'age of the child', the reasoning is usually quite different even when the conclusions are the same. That is why the discussion of children in this book is reserved for the next chapter.

The Renaissance and the Reformation made little difference. When John Colet lectured to the University of Oxford on I Corinthians at the end of the fifteenth century, he expressed in gentle and urbane words the old sentiments of the more violent Fathers: marriage was second-best, having nothing good in itself save only in so far as it provided a remedy for a necessary evil. It restrained and confined the lawlessness of venereal desire. Man's weakness had extracted from an indulgent God the use of wives and matrimony, but the true ideal was that of masculine continence. Actually, these questions did not excite much learned controversy during the Reformation. The sixteenth-century reformers were on the whole concerned with practical matters, but sexually conservative, appealing to scripture and for that very reason sometimes productive of especially reactionary attitudes. In theory they were content to oppose obligatory vows of continence and to affirm the honesty of wedlock, even though its sacramental character was repudiated. It is, of course, dangerous to raise speculations about psychology and to do so provides an easy target for ridicule, but it is perhaps permissible for the historian to wonder whether the age of the Reformation did not usher in an even more horrified attitude towards sex, or at least its aberrations, than had existed in the fifteenth century. This remark is ventured through comparing the growing superstitions about sorcery and witchcraft from the fifteenth century onwards: in the fifteenth century most recorded cases appear to have political overtones, whereas in the sixteenth and seventeenth centuries witches, *incubi* and *succubi* might be held as the projection of sexual fantasies by a society deeply alarmed in its sexual being.

Apart from this, more attention was slowly being paid to parenthood after the Reformation. Calvin was suspicious of pleasure and saw matrimony as primarily social rather than generative, and an institution ruled by the father. A dominant puritanism now brought with it a social rather than an ascetic goal. Post-medieval ideas of marriage are more closely linked than before to the idea of society as a whole and, whatever their scriptural ferocity, possess their tender and appealing side for the modern mind. Thomas Becon in the seventeenth century bade Wootton look forward to the time when 'some little young babe shall play in your hall . . . which with mild lisping or amiable stammering shall call you Dad'. This is not a medieval voice.

(b) The business of medieval marriage

The usual view of marriage in the western world today is a romantic one. This means, as everyone knows, that the main acceptable reason for getting married is 'being in love' and, further, that the onslaught of this condition is both unpredictable and compulsive. Certainly, any notion of a business side to marriage, such as dowries or settlements or the mutual inspection of bank balances, is a repellent one to most contemporaries and likely to be vilified as mercenary, loveless and medieval. Yet let us not entirely deceive ourselves. Marriage never has been and never can be wholly separated from arrangements about property. For most of us, romantic marriage is thinkable simply because in an industrial society there is on the one hand sufficient personal property to allow it, in the form of wages and salaries, and, on the other hand, insufficient dynastic property in the shape of landed family estates to forbid it. When there is full employment and easy mobility there are few practical obstacles to setting up small matrimonial families. The situation is different where there is serious poverty, as in Ireland, or, conversely, where the notable wealth of social groups can be preserved and enlarged, untaxed, over a long period by marriage policy. And since literature reflects life, and contemporary literature is mainly for salary- and wage-earners, little enough is heard of the *business* of marriage. Those who set about to marry money generally keep quiet about it. Inflation and full employment have turned the *Forsyte Saga* into a historical novel, barely relevant to the lives of most of its readers.

In spite of all this, there is a usefulness in explaining the business of medieval marriage which goes beyond a remote and lifeless curiosity by calling attention to the way people lived for a long period of western history, and to the custom of the late Middle Ages. It is always necessary to fight the conception that the medievals were especially barbarous or dishonest, and if these proceedings are properly explained it helps one to understand that we are different from them for historical and not moral reasons. How different they were in their deepest hearts we can never know. The historian must be permitted to laugh and to cry, to approve or to disapprove, if he wishes to, since his feelings are essential circumstances of his art; but his understanding must first prevail.

Throughout the Middle Ages and beyond, in all classes of society, a marriage was arranged not only by the intending partners but by their families and superiors. This is a custom more strikingly different from modern Anglo-Saxon methods even than the bargaining about property that was allied with it. Among peasant families, fathers and mothers, or uncles and elder brothers, or a semi-professional village match-maker, were required to initiate courtships. The son could not support a wife and children on nothing. He needed either his father's holding, or part of it, or new land if there were any, or to live in dependence for a time on his father with his father's consent, before he got married. The family looked about them for a suitable match for son or daughter, or considered the suggestion of the son himself, and the family then dispatched a go-between, an intermediate or 'mean' person to make a proposal to the girl's family that the couple might become more thoroughly acquainted. Of course, there were many variations on this theme, but *Piers Plowman* in late fourteenth-century England described a common form:

> And thus was wedlock y-wrought with a mean person:
> First by father's will and the friends' counsel,

89

> And then by assent of themselves, as the two might accord;
> And thus was wedlock y-wrought, and God himself it made.*

Here are the elements, connecting the necessary assent described in the previous section with the social methods of the day.

It is not surprising that much more can be discovered in the sources about the more affluent sections of society than about simple country people, nor that, as time goes on and the documents of middling rich families become more copious, the later Middle Ages can be better known in this respect than the earlier.

In all ranks of society, surviving marriage contracts are rather rare, though less so as the fifteenth century goes on. A good early example which may be cited, in order to show that fifteenth-century practice had not changed much from that of the thirteenth century, comes from a collection of Kentish deeds belonging to the family of Peckham. The deeds themselves are smallish pieces of parchment. Pieced together in chronological order, these documents display a fairly well-to-do landowning family building up its possessions in north Kent in the thirteenth century, and its members can be traced in wills and other documents into modern times.

The first clear view is of Martin Peckham, who in 1282 drew up a contract for his own marriage with Margery, daughter of another local notability called Henry of Shorne.† Martin must have been of relatively mature age and economically independent at the time, for he had bought a new house seven years earlier at Yaldham, near Sevenoaks. Shorne, where his prospective father-in-law lived, is a village near Rochester, a few miles away. Henry of Shorne came over to Martin's house and pledged himself under oath to pay Martin 'for the sake of matrimony' the then large sum of £53. 6s. 8d. over four years in six-monthly instalments, every November and June, promising also a penalty sum of £2 each time he fell into arrears. There were further guarantees of the payment, which might lead to loss of property if he defaulted, and even to ecclesiastical sanctions against him. It all sounds very severe, but it was in reality a quite ordinary series of guarantees for a business contract.

The marriage in due course took place, and Margery bore her husband children called John, William, Henry, Alexander, Alice and Isabel. Much later in history the family sense of the Peckhams seems so pronounced that it amounted to eccentricity. For Reynold Peckham, who died in 1523, was

*The Vision of Piers the Plowman, edited by W. Skeat, Text B, Passus IX, lines 113—16 (modernized).

†British Museum, Additional Charter 16503.

clearly a bachelor or a childless widower who left everything to his collateral kinsmen; yet in his will he wrote.

> ... Also I will that myn executours shall provide a faire stone with the pictures of a man and of a woman and of children therein sett of latyn [latten], and hyt to be laide over and upon my grave within the space of six weeks next immediately after my decesse. . . .*

The phrasing is conclusive that what he desired was this kind of tomb and not the commemoration of an actual family he had once had; the vague instruction is a warning against too firm a reliance upon church memorial tablets or brasses as precise genealogical evidence. It may also suggest a high value set at that time upon children, when England was just beginning to recover from a hundred years of depleted population, and when, as will be seen in the next chapter, a more special attention was beginning to be paid to the education of children and their existence as an integral part of the family circle.

Formal marriage contracts were drawn up by local scribes or notaries who knew how to do these things in proper form and were naturally paid for their services. By the late fifteenth and early sixteenth centuries many were made which have survived. Just one example may be cited (though it comes from as late as 27 April 1547) because it refers to the wedding reception as well as to the long-term property arrangements.† Written in English, as they mostly were by now, it promises that Richard Hoo, esquire of Norfolk, shall marry off his daughter Joan to Humfrey Dean, gentleman, also of Norfolk. In consideration of this, the marriage was to be solemnized before the coming Michaelmas at the parish church of Scarning. Richard was to make and provide 'an honest and convenient repast or dyner the day of the solempnization of the seid espousallez or marriage, with lodgeng, meat and drinke for the aliez, frendez and kynesfolkez of the same Richard and Humfrey, soo long as they or eny of them shall be contentid reasonablie to tarie and abide at the mansion hous of the seid Richard at Scarning'. Joan was to be clothed at her father's cost 'accordyng to her pore degree and behaviour'. Before the feast, Humfrey was to assure lands of his inheritance to the value of £8 a year to Joan and her assigns for life. Richard was to pay Humfrey £53 6s. 8d., by four instalments over a year, starting at once, each payment to be made upon the font stone in the parish church between 2 and 3 o'clock in the after-

*Somerset House, will register 'Bodfelde', folio 31.
†Public Record Office, Ancient Deeds, A 13522. I owe this and many similar references to the kindness of Mr R. W. Dunning.

noon. In guarantee of this Richard was to make over land worth 45s. a year till the debt was paid.

By the fifteenth century this kind of formal record has been reinforced by numerous private letters, of which the Paston collection is the best known. These open to us the minds and hearts of men and women better than the official documents can ever do. In 1453 Margaret Paston wrote to her husband John, who was in London, 'my mother prayeth you to remember my sister and to do your part faithfully before you come home to help to get her a good marriage. . . . It is said that Knyvet the heir wants to marry; both his wife and child are dead. She wishes you to enquire if this is so, and what his livelihood is, and, if you think there is some possibility, to have him spoken with . . . '*

The letter alludes to 'livelihood', the common fifteenth-century term for property, especially landed property. Its mention here makes it suitable to embark upon the general discussion of property in marriage, even though at times the discussion will have to be technical and possibly tedious.

Many people in medieval England held at least part of their property in feudal (that is, military, or knightly) tenure, in distinction from both unfree tenure and the free but non-knightly tenures generically known as *socage*. This did not at all necessarily mean that such tenants in the later Middle Ages were knights, though they may have been so. But it did mean that the chief lord of whom they held the land had the right to give the heir in marriage. He could make money out of this, especially if the inheritance were a rich one, for eligible people were naturally glad to marry someone well-to-do and would pay for the lord's consent to such a marriage. It was perhaps the surest way of making a capital gain. The monarch in particular derived a fair income by exercising this right of Wardship and Marriage, whether it was a twelfth-century king, noting his rights in a systematic 'Roll of Ladies and Boys in the king's gift', kept in his Exchequer, or whether it was Queen Elizabeth I, profiting from the 'Queen's Wards'.

The bulk of a family's resources was in land, and wardship and marriage rights were means by which landholders could make a profit out of the system. Inheritances had to be kept together, if possible, so that the family could go on existing in its wealth and respectability and not be reduced to poverty by the dissipation of its estates. This was as true of the country gentry as of the king. It mattered whom your children and also your tenants married. There was always a tendency for portions of the property to

---

Paston Letters, ɪ, No. 185. The text has been modernized. The Paston women's spelling and syntax are often somewhat obscure.

get broken off and lost, not only by violence and lawsuits, but by gifts to
non-inheriting younger children or gifts or sales to religious houses or to
other people. Consequently, even to maintain a family inheritance in its
integrity, it was wise for a man to marry a woman who would bring something new, if not more land at least some money or goods with which house
could be set up, more land bought, younger children as well as the eldest son
provided for. If she enlarged the estate by being an heiress in her own right,
so much the better. Lords of land in feudal tenure therefore held on to their
right to have a lucrative say in the marriage of the heir; where lands were
held in socage, the family itself were tenacious in keeping their right to consent to suitable marriages and to enjoy the profits of land which would pass
to young children when they came to their majority.

There is another very important point. Medieval people had no very acute
understanding of economic theory, but it was apparent enough, at least
from about 1200 onwards, that the value of money was tending to fall, sometimes fast, sometimes slowly, sometimes generally, and sometimes just in
relation to certain goods like manufactured articles. At the same time, in a
customary, agrarian society, rents tended to be traditional and fixed. Land-
owners could not raise their rents and taxes quickly and easily and at their
own sweet will. If they wanted a hedge against inflation they needed property
of real value, and this basically meant 'real property', or land. This is why
the rights of wardship and marriage were so important. They represented
the income from land and its produce, the value of which kept better pace
with the rise in prices than mere fixed rents; and the sale of marriages and
the enjoyment of lands of children in wardship were freely negotiable in
economic terms. This, then, is a basic condition governing medieval marriage
customs. It also explains why in a landed society there was still some suspicion about trade and merchants, which was only slowly being broken
down. Landed people were willing enough to countenance marriage into a
mercantile family if there was obviously a good deal of wealth available
to rescue or improve their fortunes, and this happened often enough. But
there was even then some social snobbery about 'trade', and there was also a
certain uneasiness about wealth which came through commercial enterprise
and which might be blown away by a gale of misfortune. Business profits
were not exactly 'livelihood' in the safest and more ancient sense. 'There is
a young man,' wrote a correspondent of Sir William Plumpton in 1464, 'a
mercer in the Cheap, who at Michaelmas proposes to set up a shop of his
own, and who makes great labour . . . for my sister Isabel to marry with her.
Livelihood he has none . . . what he is worth in goods I cannot tell. Mercers

do not deal altogether with their own goods.'* It is no wonder that merchants felt the need for land and invested in it when they could.

When marriage settlements were made, a whole series of rules and customs about land and property had to be applied. European families were kept together by the principle of male succession. Most often, the eldest son inherited the bulk of the land and the younger ones had to seek their fortune in other ways. In general, the higher men rose in the social and economic scale, the greater emphasis they placed upon the main inheritance passing to the eldest son. Likewise, of course, in a patrilinear society, children tended to take the name of their father: John son of Walter, FitzWalter, Watson, Watkin, Watkinson. Likewise again, the girl at marriage entered her husband's family. In such a society the family looks back to the male ancestor. It was common both to the Roman and Germanic worlds, it was a fundamental principle which shaped their laws about land and property, and it implied the dominance of the husband in handling the family's wealth.

In England, the common law about married women was not really crystallized until somewhere about 1250. By then it was agreed that a husband could sell or give his own landed property without reference to his wife, and could do the same with his wife's landed property if he could show her consent. He was thought of as the guardian of her property even though she had certain rights. Quite the most important of these married woman's rights was dower. This was the right of a woman after the death of her husband to a settled proportion — rarely less than a third — of all the lands he had ever possessed during their marriage. This third she must be allowed to enjoy during her widowhood, though at her death it had to revert to the family. Nothing was allowed to interfere with this. Magna Carta in 1215 had forbidden that a widow should be made to pay for her dower and had insisted that she should be allowed to stay within the matrimonial home for forty days, during which her dower should be assigned to her. If the home happened to be a castle, and therefore wanted at once, she must be found a dower house and provided with enough to live on. The same rules applied in the simplest village during the Middle Ages, and the testaments of husbands can be found in plenty arranging such matters. When Thomas Hall, yeoman of Bexley in Kent, made his will in 1527, his mother as well as his wife was still alive, and he made provision for Joan, his widow, to have certain lands in a near-by village and then, when his mother died, Joan was to move into the principal dower house in Bexley. The widow had to maintain her dower

*Plumpton Correspondence, p. 11.

property suitably, and she had to give it up if she married again.* The same year Alice Swetesyre of North Cray, near Bexley, was assigned dower by her dying husband, 'and she with myn executours to see the innyng of all my corne, and at Michaelmas she to departe out of the said house laufully with all suche legacies and bequests as to hir before is gevyn and lymyted'.†

It may seem odd that the common law of England protected the widow's right to her landed dower but offered her no similar protection for the personal property she had brought to the marriage. But the English common lawyers had decided that husband and wife during their lives together did *not* possess community of ownership. In any case, jurisdiction over personal property bequeathed in testaments fell to the church courts, so that the common law had no say in their disposition. Between the two kinds of law, married women failed to gain any legal control over their personal belongings. To marry a man was in theory for the girl to make him a gift of all she possessed. In actuality, all this was quite academic. Husbands can be seen bequeathing their widows large amounts of personal property, and they often specify those things which their wives had brought to the marriage. Alice Swetesyre, met above, was to have 'all her wearing gear' except one girdle which had belonged to her husband's first wife, and all 'the stuff of household which she brought to me at the time of her marriage', though the hangings and bedsteads in their matrimonial home were to remain when Alice moved off into the dower house. Also, many married women carried on trades on their own account, and the courts in practice allowed them to dispose of their property by will. It was never authoritatively stated that a woman might *not* dispose of goods by testament, even though legal theory regarded everything as within the husband's right during marriage.

It will easily be seen, therefore, that from the viewpoint of the law of property, the best times of a woman's life were (if she had any property) before marriage and during widowhood. But in real life the full vigour of the law's letter can rarely have been effective, and historical sources show married women almost as much in free control of personal property as they are today.

Here, to take a single illustration, are some of the sentiments from an English didactic verse of the fifteenth century, entitled *How the Good Wife Taught her Daughter*:‡

*Somerset House, will register 'Porch', folio 20.
†ibid., folio 23.
‡*Manners and Morals in Olden Time*, edited by F. J. Furnivall (1868), pp. 36—47.

95

If you want to be a good wife, pay your tithes, care for the poor, give freely, don't gad about town or get drunk on your clothing money, or at least don't get drunk often. Pay your people their wages promptly and be generous. Be hospitable, but don't ruin your husband with extravagance, especially if he's poorly off. When your daughters are born, begin to collect things for their marriages.

The literature of manners and the evidence of hundreds of testaments show women of the later Middle Ages in full charge of the household economy and often as dominant agents in the family business. The Paston correspondence is full of such instances, as when in 1453 Margaret wrote to her husband telling him how she had bargained for a lease with one Newman. Newman wanted £3 6s. 8d., but Margaret wanted to give no more than £3, though in the end she agreed to pay the extra 6s. 8d. out of her own purse, telling Newman that her husband was not to know.*

Yet because the law regarded the husband as dominant and the wife reduced to childlike dependence, the literature of courtly love sometimes took marriage as the shocking reversal of a noble relationship; for the love viewed in courtly imagination as the source of all beauty in life and manners, because freely given by the lady, became after marriage not a free gift (which only a superior can award) but a duty of obedience from one who has sunk from lady into mere woman.

When the moment came to make a marriage, the negotiations began. Perhaps it should be repeated that the girl had generally to like her suitor, though even on her part the liking was often not unmixed with an appraisal of his property. 'My cousin Clare,' wrote Agnes Paston about a possible suitor, 'thinks it would be folly to forsake him unless you know of another as good or better ... and I found her never so willing as she is to him, if it is really so that his land is unencumbered.'† When the contract came to be drawn up, there was a great variety of possible arrangements, but two main questions stood out. What will the girl's father give as a marriage portion with his daughter? And what will the bridegroom, or his father, settle on the couple? These are the two main ingredients of a marriage contract, and they are to be found in societies all over the world. The transaction was not one between two individuals but between two groups. The terms used to distinguish these transactions were sometimes used indiscriminately, so it is important to be clear about things and not just names. From the woman's side, it was not unusual in the earlier Middle Ages to provide some land,

*Paston Letters, I, No. 189.
†ibid., No. 70; cf. No. 197.

settled on the wife by her family. This was the *maritagium* of which Magna Carta speaks, and which she is to have again if her husband dies first. The text seems also to call it her inheritance (*hereditas*). But by the fourteenth century the *maritagium* had become the marriage-portion and was generally (though not always) a sum of money, paid by the bride's father. Great men might pay as much as £600 or £1,000; the gentry of the fifteenth century might expect to pay £100 or less. As we have seen, payment was not infrequently in instalments, and deposited in a religious house as though it were a bank. There were many girls whose families were not rich enough to provide much if anything, and a standard work of piety was to leave a bequest by testament 'for poor maidens' marriages'; such money was often administered in the parish by the churchwardens, who were becoming influential figures.

Fathers sometimes specified that their unmarried daughters were to have a certain sum if they decided to enter a religious order instead of marrying. James Peckham, esquire, who died in 1532 left £100 to each of his daughters when they reached the age of twenty-two or else married, whichever was the earlier. Till then, they were to be kept or otherwise provided for 'as by putting them to service'. But if one became a nun she was to have only £26 13s. 4d., to be paid part on her entry and part at her profession.* The fact that it came somewhat cheaper to make her a nun than a wife was common experience in England and in Europe in the late Middle Ages and early modern period, and resulted in numerous 'false vocations' and in unhappiness which can be felt across the centuries if not measured by any historian.

From the man's side must come the whole prospect of a decent 'livelihood', out of which the woman's position had to be safeguarded in case he died first. In the early Middle Ages the rules about this also were not firm, and precise arrangements had to be made before witnesses at the church door. There the bridegroom gave his bride gold and silver, not as spending money but as a pledge of her endowment, her dowry should he die, and such a pledge was called the *wed*. Only after the wedding did the people go inside the church for the nuptial mass. The Magna Carta reissue of 1217 refers to the possibility of arranging a dowry at the church door — *ad ostium ecclesiae*. If this were not done, it was assumed the widow would get her third part. In the later Middle Ages, this settlement of property upon the wife was usually called her jointure. It was likely to be capital property, like land or a rent-

---

*Somerset House, will register 'Thower', folio 23.

income, settled on the wife by the husband, or on both of them by the husband's father, with reversion to the heirs of their union or back to the husband's family if the marriage proved sterile. Sometimes too the wife renounced her arranged dowry in return for a specific bequest.

It had, of course, long been possible for a married couple to receive an estate in entail, that is, property which they could not legally dispose of by sale or gift and which had to descend to the children or, more likely, to the eldest boy. This was called property in 'fee tail' as distinct from 'fee simple'. As we shall see,* the ingenuity of lawyers was such that by the fifteenth century men had learned how to break entails in order to dispose of such land as they wished. They had wanted to do this even in the thirteenth century, though one of Edward I's statutes had tried to stop it.† The fifteenth century was even more an age of social and economic mobility and varied family ambitions, and legal technique favoured family flexibility.

It was for these reasons that the actual wedding was a rapid and business-like ceremony which took place outside the church or, as now, before the altar rails, and only after it was over did the couple move inside the sanctuary to hear the nuptial mass from their fald-stools.

We do not possess many accounts of actual marriage ceremonies from the Middle Ages, apart, of course, from the ritual forms in service books and in church statutes. One occurs in a legal document from thirteenth-century Warwickshire,‡ in which a priest testified to the marriage of a couple which he remembered. He swore that on Wednesday, 21 August 1241, he was present in the conventual church of Cook Hill, Worcestershire, between 9 a.m. and 3 p.m., when John Giffard, in the face of the church and the presence of the witness himself, who was officiating, was asked if he agreed to take Aubrée de Caumvill for his lawful wife, to have and to hold before all others; and he answered that he did. Likewise, Aubrée, being asked if she consented, answered that she did. After this, John took Aubrée from the hand of the witness, saying, 'I take thee to my lawful wife, to have and to hold all the days of my life.' And so they mutually plighted their troth (*se affidaverunt*). Then, taking the blessed ring from the priest's hand, John espoused (*subarravit*) Aubrée, saying, 'With this ring I thee wed, with my body and goods I thee honour.' After this the mass was solemnized, and he then led her back to

---

*Below, p. 121
†Namely, the section of the Second Statute of Westminster (1285) known as *De Donis Conditionalibus* (*Statutes of the Realm*, vol. I, p. 71).
‡*Calendar of Inquisitions post mortem*, vol. XIII, No. 313.

Left A fifteenth-century wedding. *Right* The wedding of Henry V and Catherine of France, 2 June 1420.

the town of Arrow in Warwickshire from which he had brought her, with a great company to feast with them.

The crowd of guests and spectators at weddings, always traditional, was naturally not only the sign of family rejoicing and the excuse for a party, but basically the means by which witnesses were provided to an act which could, in the eyes of the Church, be validly performed in complete privacy but which, without witnesses, could be denied later by one or both parties who might want to split up and contract other marriages. Church pronouncements were constantly read out from pulpits against clandestine marriages which in this way could so easily lead on to adulteries and the procreation of illegitimate children in a society where divorce in the modern sense of the term was regarded as impossible and children could not be legitimized by the subsequent marriage of their parents.

When we reflect upon the business aspect of marriage contracts — the money and the lands contributed from either side — it is obvious that some interesting problems call for further thought. Did it, for instance, cost a father more to get his daughter married than to endow his son's marriage? At what age did most men and women get married? How many remarriages were there after the death of one of the parties? Medieval documents do not provide enough evidence to supply any exact answers to questions such as these, but that is no reason for refusing to wonder about them, and every now and then scraps of information appear which enable one to guess at some solution. One of the most hopeful lines of approach is to look at the demo-

graphic and economic trends: that is to say, the total population, its proportion to the amount of wealth available, and the ratio of men to women. It has been shown that thirteenth-century England was overpopulated in relation to the land available, and suggested that in some areas young men desperate for a foothold on land would gladly marry fairly senior widows for the sake of their property, which would be enjoyed by their second or subsequent husbands. When these widows died, the widower could then look round for an attractive young girl, who in turn would ultimately be left a widow, so that landed property in a fully populated place like Taunton in Somerset might see-saw between widows and widowers to the detriment of the children. On the other hand, poverty precludes marriage, and there must also have been many unmarried people of quite advanced age, as in the Ireland of more modern times. By the fifteenth century, the fall in population and the rise in real wages suggests that marriage would be easier for more people at an earlier age. This is not easy to prove directly. In later medieval London the marriage-rate was certainly high, but the age at marriage does not appear to have been notably low, as often happens when marriage is easier. This may have been attributable to the special circumstances of a merchant society which demanded suitable disposition of property. Few instances can be found of boys of the merchant class marrying under the age of twenty-one (though even now this is considered quite young for a man), and many wills left money to be delivered to sons at ages between twenty and twenty-four or 'when married', which reasonably allows the inference that these were likely ages of marriage. Occasionally, even the age of twenty-six was demanded for boys. Probably girls of this class married younger than the men, perhaps at seventeen or so. Kentish wills give the impression that fifteenth-century girls of moderately prosperous parents married when they were between the ages of eighteen and twenty-one. What is clear is that the families which have left any records at all were eager to get the daughters married off. The Pastons liked to get the girls placed in service in great households, where they had to be well clothed, in the hope of marriage prospects.*
Sir John Paston, who was in some financial difficulties in 1470, wanted to get rid of Anne Paston, who had been living in his household, and get her married, as 'she is getting tall'.† Some families felt strongly that daughters should be married in order of age,‡ though naturally this did not always occur.

The comparative costs of a son's and a daughter's marriage cannot be

*_Paston Letters_, II, No. 601 (1469).
†ibid., No. 660.
‡_Stonor Letters_, No. 54 (1431).

reckoned, at least until more research has been done. Circumstances differ so much that it is even hard to decide what 'cost' was, since the marriage of a son or a daughter might prove a good family investment of the sum involved. The impression remains, however, that the girl's marriage was more of a worry than the boy's to the parents, since the young man almost by definition had to bear the cost of livelihood himself and was not the dependent partner; he was, moreover, the asker and not the asked. The bride's father may therefore have been thankful enough to obey the traditional dictates of custom which required him to support the wedding feast, cheered by the thought that the clothes and expensive feminine requirements of his daughter would in future be taken care of by another man.

(c) Love and sex

Much of this discussion has been about the legal and economic sides of marriage, but it would be historically incomplete to end the chapter without turning for a moment to those more delicate and personal realities with which the historian must also deal, even if by so doing he is attempting to measure the unmeasurable or resurrect secrets which even contemporaries could hardly have guessed. Of happiness no one can speak with certainty, save perhaps within the close circle of living intimates, and even face to face by the firelight there exists no standard of this quality, which all feel but none in full can communicate. We must remain content with external indications.

The Italian visitor who cast an amused but inaccurate eye over the English scene about 1500 had this to say:

> Although their dispositions are somewhat licentious, I never have noticed anyone, either at court or amongst the lower orders, to be in love; whence one must necessarily conclude, either that the English are the most discreet lovers in the world, or that they are incapable of love. I say this of the men, for I understand it is quite contrary with the women, who are very violent in their passions. Howbeit, the English keep a very jealous guard over their wives, though anything may be compensated in the end, by the power of money.*

These remarks may be the merest reportage, but the same observer was sufficiently precise about mercantile marriages to make his comments on love at least worth noting.

Medieval marriage without romance or sexual love appears an all too frequent likelihood, but the fact cannot have been universal. Child marriages were in the main confined to higher political realms. Arranged marriages

*For the source of this extract, see p. 25 above.

are not necessarily sad. Also, a girl could be defiant in defence of her heart:

> I wish you would speak with Weeks and know his disposition to Jane Walsham [wrote Margaret Paston to Sir John in 1463]. She hath said since he went away that unless she might have him she would never be married, her heart is sore set on him. She told me that he said to her that there was no woman in the world he loved so well. I hope he is not deceiving her. . . .*

Another possibility: love may grow after marriage if thought and prudence have been exercised before it. One need not here confine speculation to any particular class of society. Possibly the naturalness of choice became more free and flexible as one descended the scale of wealth. Possibly 'middle-class' girls of families on the make suffered more than most. For every Margery who stood out for her low-born Richard Calle, there may have been many Annes: 'Take good heed to my sister Anne,' wrote Sir John Paston in 1473, who wanted to marry her off to the judge Yelverton, 'lest the old love between her and Pampyng renew.† Yet some girls learned that they must learn to love, after all was sealed and signed.

> And if it like your good motherhood to hear of me and how I do [wrote Elizabeth after her eventual marriage to Robert Poynings, achieved after a host of stormy courtships], at the making of this letter I was in good health of body, thanked be Jesu. And as for my master, — my best beloved that ye call — and I must needs call him so now, for I find no other cause, . . . he is full kind unto me.‡

Glimpses here and there show the relationship blossoming. Margaret, the most lovable of all the Paston characters, wrote with painful spelling to her new husband, again and again 'desiring heartily to hear of your welfare', and pouring out her insistence that she 'was not in her heart's ease from the time that she knew of his sickness until she knew verily of his mending'.§ From the husband's side, too, the correspondence of the fifteenth century is rich in demonstration of attraction, love and happiness. A man had eyes and tongue to praise what he saw.‖ The worldly Sir John Paston read Ovid's *De Arte Amandi*, was praised as 'the best chooser of a gentlewoman', and advised his brother on the skills of wooing;** and Friar Brackley, preach-

Paston Letters, II, No. 480.
†ibid., III, No. 732.
‡ibid., I, No. 322.
§ ibid., No. 36.
‖ ibid., II, No. 479.
¶ibid., No. 568.
**ibid., No. 570.

ing on the stability of perfect joy, could take married love for a figure, though, as he reflected, 'mutable as a shadow' and incomparable with everlasting bliss.*

A circumstantial account of a courtship's beginning occurs in the *Cely Papers*,† and it revivifies before our eyes the gentle hesitations and coquetries which no property deal could mask or obliterate:

Right entirely beloved brother [wrote Richard Cely in May 1482], the same day that I came to Northleach on a Sunday before Matins from Burford, William Midwinter welcomed me and in our communication he asked me if I were in any way of marriage. I told him nay, and he informed me that there was a young gentlewoman whose father's name is Lemryke and her mother is dead and she shall inherit £40 a year as they say in that country, and her father is the greatest ruler as richest man in that country.... [I was told] if I would tarry till May Day I should have a sight of the young gentlewoman, and I said I would tarry with a goodwill.... To Matins the same day came the young gentlewoman and her mother-in-law [stepmother?], and I and William Bretten were saying Matins when they came into church. And when Matins were done they went to a kinswoman of the young gentlewoman and I sent them half a gallon of white romnay, and they took it thankfully, for they had come a mile on foot that morning. And when Mass was done I came and welcomed them and kissed them and they thanked me for the wine and prayed me to come to dinner with them, and I excused me and they made me promise to drink with them after dinner; and I sent them to dinner a gallon of wine, and they sent me a heron [roast?]; and after dinner I came and drank with them and took William Bretten with me, and we had right good talk, and the person pleased me well, as by the first communication she is young, little and very well-favoured and witty, and the country speaks much good by her. Sir, all this matter abideth the coming of her father to London, that we may understand what sum he will give as a marriage portion, and how he likes me. He will be here within three weeks. I pray send me a letter how you think by this matter....

These were the normalities of courtship and marriage, but twentieth-century readers will inevitably wonder about the reverse side of the medal, suspicious in all fairness that a world where romance took very much a second place outside literature must have compensated itself in hidden ways for the joyless routine of supervised match-making. Even in far-away Romagna romantic love seemed an enemy to the poet Pietro Francesco, whose peasant in the *Commedia Nuova* told in Romagnol dialect how he managed against odds to capture and bind love:

Paston Letters, I, No. 372.
†*Cely Papers*, No. 89. This translation into modern English is based on that of J. J. Bagley, *Historical Interpretation*, Penguin Books, 1965, pp. 180–1.

el traditore
che tradisse tutta la gente,

and how the captor would release him only for cash and not for kisses:

An dighe a cusì ie o cantarin
A dighe bisogna quatrin quatrin
e no bese. . . . *

Here in England the rules were clear, and written with prime insistence, as today, in manuals for confessors where lust appears the deadliest and universal enemy of God. But equally clearly the rules were, as in all ages, broken. Were they broken more often then than at other historical periods? Were they broken in ways special to the times? Did their breaking attract great or mild social opprobrium? All answers are guesswork, and a few illustrations must suffice to encourage the reader's judgement. French and German historians have stigmatized the fifteenth century as 'the age of bastards'. In the region of Bordeaux bastards were an accepted part of the scene in noble households. Usually they were bequeathed capital sums of money, or pensions; sometimes they were even left fiefs by means of which they might attain nobility. Later medieval France has many examples of illegitimate sons of the nobility achieving brilliant careers in ecclesiastical or military life, though perhaps few aristocrats displayed the splendid insouciance of the Vicomte de Castelbon in the Béarn, who left sums of money to each of his bastards 'already born or yet to be born'.† This is a subject where the truth seems always to vary according to whether it deals with the rich, the poor or the middling classes. *Bürgerlich* morals tend to be stricter than those of the rich or the poor, and one may give to this supposition social and economic explanations: the need to keep up appearances in a world of ambitious competition, allied with the limited means available for such appearances. Even today, divorce appears simpler both for the well-to-do and those poor enough to enjoy legal aid at the state's expense, and who have little to lose, than for the middle classes among whom scandal and conscience might appear more severe realities. In medieval England, and especially London, there is enough evidence from the proceedings of ecclesiastical courts and visitations to suggest that adultery was exceedingly common, though it appears more usual among married women than unmarried girls, who, far more than today, were the closely watched property of their families. Instances will illustrate, even if they

---

*Cited by John Larner, *The Lords of Romagna* (1965), p. 121, who translates: 'I dinna say aye to that, singer lad, I say it's bawbees, bawbees, and nae' kisses, I'm wanting.'
†Robert Boutruche, *La crise d'une société* (1963), pp. 293–4.

Adultery illustrated in a hand-book of Canon Law.

cannot prove this point. At Swalecliffe in Kent the parish priest, Sir James, 'drawithe to oone Johan, Potter's wif, and she cannot be ride of hym', and he 'doethe stand herkenyng under menys wyndowes at 10 of the clock in the night.'* Also in 1511, a married man was accused of keeping another woman. failed to clear himself, and was awarded the normal penance of standing bareheaded and barefoot, in shirt and breeches only, in the local church, with a wax candle in his hands, and required to join the procession and offer the candle to the parish priest at the Sunday High Mass.† At Canterbury, Elizabeth Kirkby, lady of Horton, was warned to break off her adulterous connection with Robert Lad of Eynsford, and the clerical scribe amused himself by drawing the culprit in vermilion ink in the margin, before he wrote up the lady's absolution on the next page.‡ These are but examples from hundreds of such cases. But it is not to be forgotten that ecclesiastical courts could protect women as well as punish them. In 1490 the diocesan court of London ordered John Gunton, citizen and dyer, to pay £4 damages to the use of Elizabeth Medigo whom he had got with child. In 1526 a defendant called William Anderson was told to treat his wife with marital affection, to pay the rent, to give her 4d. a week, and to cohabit with her on festal days and when his occupation allowed him to do so.

In a society where social and religious pressures insisted so rigidly upon holding together the matrimonial alliance, the existence of brothels as well as adulterous connections between married people calls for no surprise. London, and especially Southwark, had its stews: much of this quarter was under the jurisdiction either of the Archbishop of Canterbury or the Bishop of Winchester, and the ladies of light virtue who inhabited it were sometimes known as 'Winchester geese'. Ecclesiastical records provide some detail. In

*Register of Archbishop Warham (Lambeth Palace), folio 47.
†ibid., folios 47v., 62.
‡*Historical Manuscripts Commission, Eighth Report, Part I*, Appendix (1881), p. 337a, from Canterbury Cathedral Register G.

1493 Nan Hooper was charged before the Bishop of London's Official with perjury for not fulfilling her promise to marry Thomas Pollardson. She was said to pass many nights in the stews, and the echoes of a virago's voice come down to us through the formal records: 'cursse and bliss', she answered the court, 'I sett not a straw by the cursing there'.* Counteracting these small motions of permissiveness, London also shows a growing streak of rigorism among the lower middle classes of artisans, some of whom were touched by the new Lollardy, which tended to be anti-permissive in questions of sexual morals and hostile to ecclesiastical courts for their failure to repress as well as for their existence itself. When John of Northampton became mayor in October 1381, there was a strong 'clean up the city' campaign. Northampton was said (improbably) to have Lollard leanings, but he was bitterly attacked for his anti-ecclesiastical activity.† Real Lollards held very strong views about sex. Their manifesto in London in 1395 contained the propositions that celibacy was impossible and led to unnatural vice, and that the religious profession of widows was especially harmful, in that it encouraged promiscuity, forms of birth-control, infanticide and abortion among many who were unfaithful to their vows. Mixed up with this were feelings of hatred for luxuries and unnecessary possessions made by goldsmiths and armourers. The manifesto appears obsessive.

In the English countryside there was less of the 'puritan' rigidity and cynicism. But manorial court rolls are full of records of small penalties levied against women, 'because she has given birth' (*quia peperit*). Here perhaps the tone, the social pressure, the fear of 'what the neighbours would say' was more firmly set by the married women than by other groups, and by modern comparison this would seem a psychological likelihood if not a truism. Edmund Paston took a sad view of his mother's insistence on the proprieties when he had to dismiss one of his servants whom he liked, but he had to obey:

> ... my mother hath caused me to put Gregory out of my service as, God help, I write to you the very cause why. It happed him to have a knave's lust, in plain terms to *swhyve a quene*, and so he did in Konynesclosse [a field]. It fortuned him to be espied by two ploughmen of my mother's ... wherefore there is no remedy but he must go. ... ‡

None the less, loyalty persisted in Edmund's heart, and he begged his brother to find Gregory another place and 'be the better master to him

*W. H. Hale (ed.), *A Series of precedents and proceedings ... extracted from Act books of ecclesiastical courts in the diocese of London* (London, 1847).
†*Historia Anglicana* II, 65; Ranulf Higden, *Polychronicon* IX, 29.
‡*Paston Letters*, I, No. 58.

for my sake, for I am as sorry to part from him as any man alive from his servant, and he is as true as any alive'.

Such an instance is a warning that the apparent man's world of the later Middle Ages was not wholly so, when the fear-driven anger of the married woman could command such force.

The lot of the illegitimate child was as bad or worse in England then than it is now. Continental law might allow the legitimation of children by the subsequent marriage of their parents, but the barons of England had refused to countenance this as long ago as 1235 – 'We do not wish the laws of England to be changed' – and social attitudes on this matter did not catch up with the development of society until the 1960s. Bastards are fairly often referred to in fifteenth-century testaments, but they could not share in any common-law inheritance. They might hope for a legacy, like John, referred to by James Peckham in 1400 as 'my bastard son called Wrotham' (where he was born), who was left 40s.* Richard Bamme, esquire, member of a wealthy city family, could afford to be more generous to 'Thomas Bishop my bastard son', for he left him £20 in 1452 'to promote him to some useful craft which he may happen to like'.† Only occasionally can the new flexibility in handing down property be found working to the advantage of illegitimate children, so that the case of William Holt, esquire of Cheshire, who died in 1487, has an interest marked by rarity value. His marriage was evidently in collapse, and before he died he arranged that his executors should allow lands worth £2 13s. 4d. to each of his five illegitimate children for their lifetimes, while his widow was to have £6 13s. 4d. He evidently had legitimate heirs as well and he spoke of the possibility of remarriage if his wife should die before him.‡

Was it then a man's world in such respects, or a woman's world? Undoubtedly, for the unmarried girl, it was an age of protection and subjection, where choice was a matter of luck, and love had to be fought for or abandoned with wry hopes for the future. For the married woman affection and perhaps a tranquil and unpassioned love came more often than not; command over households and power over behaviour certainly accompanied the married state. For the widow, the evidence speaks with more than usually conflicting voices. An educated Bohemian gentleman of the late fourteenth century, called Thomas of Stitny, thought the widowed state a good one:

I always remember how sometimes when I thought of marrying I paid no attention to what I heard from childhood from my grandmother, who was a very

*Lambeth Palace, Register of Archbishop Arundel, I, folio 176v.
†Somerset House, will register 'Rous', folio 133.
‡*Calendar of Close Rolls, 1485–1500*, No. 281.

good woman of great virtue. She used to say, 'O good Lord, how is it that widows have a greater reward than married folk? How much better and more comfortable an estate we widows have than we had in marriage!'*

Yet such matters depend upon an infinity of circumstances and are by nature subjective as well. One would do well to remember the poor widows' cottages in country villages, where they dwelt with sufficient livelihood but often in loneliness. One would do well, too, to note the distraction of Thomas Denys's wife after the murder of her husband in 1461, who prayed for a good man to protect her, and 'made such piteous moan and said that she knew not how to do for money' that Margaret Paston lent her 6s. 8d.† There are implications, again, in Thomas Walsingham's remark in 1379 when he wrote 'many widows found their way to [a nunnery] in order to become guests, as is the custom in such abbeys, either because of the neediness of their circumstances or to remain continent more perfectly and securely'.‡ Elizabeth Pole did not think her lot a truly merry one in 1504. She had been a widow for twelve years, well provided and comfortable. Now that her grandson had reached his majority she felt the call of retirement. Like so many later medieval woman, she mingled determination and business capacity with a deep piety, and longed to put off the Martha for the Mary.

Thus the matter is now [she wrote to a kinsman],§ that I have taken another house, near the friars at Derby, which is but of a small charge, and there I intend to dispose myself to serve God diligently, and keep a narrow house and but few in my household; for I have such discomfort of my son Thomas's unfortunate matters that it is time for me to get me into a little corner, and so I will do. I will beseech you and him to take no displeasure with me for my departing, for it will be not otherwise, my heart is so set. . . . I will flit at this next Michaelmas, as I am fully minded, or sooner, with God's grace. I pray you continue my good master and owe me never the worse will therefor, for it riseth on my own mind to give over great tuggs of husbandry which I had, and take me to less charge. . . .

---

*This comes from a paper read by the late Professor R. R. Betts to the Historical Congress held in Rome in 1955, printed in the Congress's *Relazioni* (Florence), volume III, p. 494.
†*Paston Letters*, II, No. 400.
‡*Historia Anglicana*, I, p. 420.
§ *Plumpton Correspondence*, pp. 190–1.

6 Household and Family

In the patrilinear, monogamous society of western Europe, marriage leads on to the setting-up of new households, either at once or within a short time. But the Middle Ages was a period of household society in a special sense, not only as a consequence of marriage and the requirements for rearing children, but because society itself in its political and religious aspects as well as its matrimonial one was formed out of innumerable households in which professionally celibate as well as married lives were lived, and from which administrative and political decisions radiated. The king's household was at the centre of government. A bishop's household was called his *'familia'*. Monasteries under their abbots or priors lived according to rules in which from time immemorial the superior took the place and the very name of father.

With these more exalted or other-worldly households we shall have little to do, apart from describing their structure, upon which lesser households were more or less modelled. For the most part, attention must be given to the households of lay men and women below royal rank, in order to see how they were composed, what rules and attitudes governed their being, and how they interacted with each other to form the society of the day.

The household of king, bishop, baron, gentleman, yeoman, or indeed of anyone with more than the barest minimum of wealth, was a centre of government, composed not only of the paterfamilias, his wife and young children, but of a crowd of dependants. All of these had to be fed, clothed, and transported. In its more elaborate form, a household was highly departmentalized. To take a single example, the Archbishop of Canterbury's household comprised a Wardrobe, Chapel, Kitchen, Pantry, Buttery, Poultery, Saucery, Scullery and Marshal's department. This organization might be changed slightly from time to time, but these departments existed in the mid fourteenth and mid fifteenth centuries, according to the scanty surviving records, and each of them had to account for the money or consumables it dispensed.* Parchment rolls recorded the expenditure, but time has made away with most of them, for they were not thought worth keeping with the same care that title-deeds to property or legal transactions merited.

In this particular household, the Wardrobe looked after expenditure incurred outside the household itself, like the bulk purchase of spices and foodstuffs, silver plates and dishes, sheets and fine furnishings, wages of messengers to near-by manor houses or to distant Rome or, to take lesser instances, the 10s. paid in 1343 to the son of the archbishop's watchman when he went off to school in Maidstone and the 1s. given to a crazy fellow who stood begging at St Thomas's shrine in Canterbury Cathedral. The internal departments of the household had to account to the Wardrobe. Of these the Kitchen was probably the biggest spender. A surprisingly high proportion of the archbishop's income was laid out on food — not only the basic requirements of butchers' meat and bread, but an almost unbelievable variety of birds and fish, many of which were brought from afar and were luxuries to the palate of the day though more or less disgusting to present tastes. Aristocratic food, at least, was often highly spiced, and much care given to its elaborate visual preparation on grand occasions. Faced with a peacock served up cooked but redressed in its original plumage, Piers Plowman would doubtless have been sarcastic. For Piers it would be more characteristic to say, in the lean days before the harvest:

I haven't a penny left, so I can't buy you pullets or geese or pigs. All I've got is a couple of fresh cheeses, a little curds and cream, an oat-cake, and two loaves of beans and bran which I baked for my children. Upon my soul, I haven't a scrap of bacon, and I haven't a cook to fry you steak and onions. But I've some parsley and shallots and plenty of cabbages, and a cow and a calf. . . . †

But the archbishop's Kitchen, catering for so many people, was an impressive affair, and on the march from one manor house to another needed a complete cart with its complement of up to six horses. Again high in financial importance came the Marshalcy, or Stabling department, which saw to the feeding and shoeing of all the horses, whether they were for riding or drawing vehicles. This transport office was housed on many of the estates in separate buildings, and even when the archbishop had leased out his estates he

*Westminster Abbey Muniments, Nos. 9222, 9223; Lambeth Palace Account Roll collection, No. 1973.
†Text B. Passus VI, lines 282—9. Translation by J. F. Goodridge (Penguin Classics, 1959), 127.

Carving at high table.

usually made arrangements for his transport in manors where he was likely to stay during his constant peregrinations. The lesser departments speak for themselves. The buttery dealt with the bottles and flagons of drink: wine for the quality and ale for everybody, and its accounts are sometimes embellished in the margin with pen-sketches of barrels. Pipes of wine containing 108 gallons each were broken down into casks at Lambeth, then decanted into flasks and drunk quickly. Wine was not then laid down for maturation. Members of the household took breakfast (*jantaculum*) privately and received daily issues of bread and drink to use as they pleased. In the Hall there were two formal meals daily: dinner (*prandium*) and supper (*cena*), and on these occasions a great household habitually entertained guests. The archbishop's household rolls are inscribed in the left-hand margin with the names of important guests and the number of attendants they brought with them, and the numbers of the *familiares*, or members of the household itself, who were present at each meal. These last were classified into the 'gentry' and the 'others', and the archbishop's household, one of the grandest in the realm, might expect twenty gentry and fifty 'others' every day to dinner and only slightly fewer to supper. Those who were not gentry (the word used in the roll is *generosi*) might be classified as yeomen or valets, assigned to various departments, and perhaps serving in a menial capacity only for a time, as young men, until they were promoted. Really menial servants would not find themselves at table with such as these.

A prelate of the church had a Chapel, which was a department of his household like any other, made mobile with cart and horses, and possessing an inventory of books, precious vessels and vestments. These should be regarded not only as liturgical equipment for the pontifical celebration of the Christian mysteries, but also as a treasure, some of which could be sold or pledged if cash had suddenly to be raised. The Chapel also contained chests of muniments and archives concerned with both the lord's estates and his spiritual functions, like lists of ordinands or books of ritual. Even a bishop might have an armoury too, complete with weapons for the defence of his retinue and property. One of the strangest differences between medieval and modern times is the undercurrent of violence with which spiritual men as well as laymen defended their rights. Local rebels or gangs who poached in an archbishop's park might be summoned and penanced for sacrilege, and they might also get broken heads or wounds from daggers and arrows. Even Oxford dons preaching suspect opinions were known at times to hurry about the lecture-halls with weapons concealed under their gowns.

Accounts from aristocratic lay households were much the same as those of high ecclesiastics. Travel occupied much of their time, mingling the pleasure of the changing scene with a discomfort that would today seem scarcely tolerable, jolting over roads which were adequate for sturdy riders but bad for carts, to arrive in some long unvisited hall where local tenants, if they were efficient, would have lit the log fires, scattered fresh rushes, and made up the beds with their coloured hangings that might please the aesthetic eye but dubiously warm a rheumatic body.

The smaller departments of a household each, of course, had responsibility for the equipment and services in its care, but special attention should be called to the late medieval age in respect of financial accounting procedures which were then developing rapidly, particularly because more and lesser people were beginning to keep their own books and rolls of income and expenditure and debts. Formal accounts were much the same as they had been since the late twelfth century: rolls of parchment on which were written the name of the accountant and the date of the financial period, followed by paragraphs itemizing arrears owing and all the sources from which the master expected his income as of right; this was followed by the expenditure which the accountant had incurred on his master's behalf, including any money handed over, and at the end a balance was struck showing how much the accountant still owed, or whether he was out of pocket, or whether, by some freak, he was exactly quit. One of the first lessons a medieval historian has to learn is that this sort of account cannot be read like a modern balance sheet, but has to be regarded as a sort of written argument. The lord claims a sum 'charged' upon his agent, and the agent then 'discharges' himself of what he has spent or handed over. Thus, the 'receipts' are

Plate 5. A fifteenth-century representation of Vincent of
                     Beauvais (thirteenth century) writing at a desk

not really receipts at all, but only claims. Two of the most obvious pitfalls are that arrears from past years are noted among 'receipts' even though they might not then or ever in fact be collected; and that the hard cash handed over to the lord or his treasurer usually appears, under the name of 'deliveries' (*liberationes denariorum*), on the 'discharge' or expenditure side. But some much more informal books or scraps of paper or parchment have survived showing that men kept private jottings of their transactions as well. Men of means were also very conscious of the need for professional assistance in their accounts. Sir John Fastolf understood this well enough, and wrote in 1457 that he must know what he could spend outside after all the necessary charges had been borne. Till this was done, he observed, a master cannot know 'whether he go backwards or forwards'.* Even so, he complained three years later that no man of worship in Norfolk had as many auditors as he, yet he could never get the certainty how his livelihood was dispensed.† In 1466 Margaret Paston told her son that his father 'in his season of trouble set more by his writings and evidence than he did by any of his moveable goods.‡ Auditors were turning into members of a well-paid profession, like today's accountants, and could ride round the country serving more than one master. When their interviewing, calculating and reporting was done, they had their own estates to return to. Such a one was George Hooton, or Howton, a gentleman of London who died in 1473 owning property there and in Kent and Wiltshire. His brother was a merchant in Worcester, and William Paston was appointed to supervise the execution of his will.§ Landlords may have leased out their great fields to yeomen and tenant farmers, but through auditors and councillors and a great apparatus of rent-collectors they still lived lives of comfort while the management and physical lordship of the soil was passing to a new class of exploiters.

Lesser households lived in lesser but similar ways, whether it were a couple of bachelor priests in Bridport with a manservant or two (their accounts have survived), or a gentleman or yeoman living in a stone or stone-and-timber or even a brick house, divided into hall, solar and kitchen. Even here they probably had more privacy than in a well-to-do merchant's house in London, where goods might be stacked up on the ground floor and the family squeezed pell-mell into a few upper rooms. It is yeomen households, perhaps, which best illustrate through surviving records the increase in personal possessions

Paston Letters, i, Nos. 304, 305.
†ibid., No. 344.
‡ibid., ii, No. 560.
§Somerset House, will register 'Wattys', folio 207.

Plate 6. The Court of King's Bench in the fifteenth century.   113
Much of its work was in the criminal law

An English bedroom of the fifteenth century, shown in a scene of the birth of Richard Beauchamp, Earl of Warwick (probably 28 February 1382).

involving at this time a wide section of the population who were neither noble nor gentle. Their testaments reveal them everywhere in the country-side, living in substantial buildings filled with 'stuff of household'. One example which may be taken is of John Hamme, a farmer at Horton Kirby in Kent, whose furniture in 1425 including the following:

in the Parlour, one long table with two pairs of trestles; another table with one pair of trestles; two forms; one iron plate for candles; one hanger and a tapestry covering for the bench in red and black; in the Pantry, one stand for ale, one hanging shelf, two other wooden shelves; in the Buttery, another stand for ale; in the principal chamber, a bed of white and black with coverlet, curtains, canvas, mattress, two blankets, one pair of sheets, a long table with a pair of trestles, a ladder. . . . *

There follow seven beds in various rooms, a ladder for the poultry, a long table of beechwood with a form in the passage by the kitchen, a long table with a pair of trestles in the Cheesehouse; in the Bakehouse, a tun for sifting meal, two kneading troughs, a board for kneading dough with a cover. There

*Stonor Letters, I, No. 50.

114

are many other implements, and reference is made to larderhouse, kitchen, stables, water-mill and cow-house.

Though he was only a yeoman, John Hamme's house was therefore comparable with a modern farmhouse and was much better equipped than the cottages of villagers and, perhaps, did we but know it, than the dwellings of some of the lesser gentry. Of these we can only confess we know little. It is even controversial at the moment how many people made up the 'average' village family. Some authorities think in terms of larger familial dwelling-groups, with aged parents and aunts and uncles under the same roof. Others are impressed by the likelihood of smaller, matrimonial families, more on today's pattern. It would seem dangerous to generalize, especially as family composition must have varied from region to region, but one cannot avoid noticing the existence of widows living alone in rural communities for which records have survived. However securely endowed they may have been, this seems a sad truth that does not alter much with the ages.

It is also difficult to generalize about the age-structure of a medium-sized household. Widows might be dowered and live elsewhere. Grown or half-grown children might be sent off elsewhere, as we shall see, and everybody wanted the girls to get married as soon as possible. Margaret Paston spoke for many when she said of her sister that 'mother was anxious to be rid of her'.* The dominant age of the household was probably partly determined by the age of its head, the father. If he were rich, important and young, it is likely that at least some of his closest servants as well as his wife and children would be young too. Indoor servants often became friends. King Richard II's unpopularity sprang partly from the natural *youth* of his chosen companions and ministers. One must not think of fifteenth-century household servants as mere domestic drudges, let alone slaves or bondmen. Hard masters there undoubtedly were, but the patriarchal tradition implied a two-way loyalty which critics of the master-servant relationship, relying on nineteenth-century experience, are prone to forget. In 1469 during hard times, John Paston asked his brother to keep six servants, even if only on a weekly basis, saying it were better to get them service in the meantime, 'as it were more worship for you than to put them from you like masterless hounds', and he would like to keep them permanently.† When a master died, it was natural to continue the old servants in their employment if possible, so we must take account of aged retainers as well as of young men newly chosen.‡

*Paston Letters, i, No. 185.
†ibid., ii, No. 631.
‡ibid., No. 561.

In the Middle Ages, little is heard of children. The family was not child-centred as it is today. It would, in fact, be impossible to entitle this chapter 'Home' because the medieval household was not home for the children as it began to be from the sixteenth century onwards. In this respect, also, the fifteenth century was an age of transition. In his brilliant book called *Centuries of Childhood*, Philippe Ariès points out that in medieval illustrations from western Europe children hardly feature even in working groups, let alone in domestic scenes, before the fifteenth century. Yet changes were on the way. To begin with, scenes of room and house interiors were becoming more common, and the popular illustrations of the year's cycle begin to show not only street and field scenes where the work of the world was carried out, but also interior furnishings, shelves, books, childbirth, deathbeds, and even the love of men and women, all set in various rooms rather than against formal flat backgrounds. England is not a promising hunting-ground for such depictions, as English painting in the fifteenth century was overshadowed first by French and then by Flemish work. But this iconography has implications for England too, and represents a new emotional tendency, directed towards the intimacy of private family life. Indeed, the very idea of the conjugal family was beginning to take the place of the older dominant concept, which stressed the hereditary line. To put it more briefly, married and family love in the present was slowly coming to mean as much as pride of dynasty. In books of etiquette, the child says grace before meals when bidden to do so by a grown-up. By the sixteenth century it was often the *youngest* child who did this. But it was not yet an age of those tender endearments, pettings and nicknames which characterize later society. Letters are addressed to 'my right worshipful father (or mother)', not to 'dear mother or *maman*'. The oldest books of courtesy spoke of children's duties to their masters rather than to their parents. The Italian who visited England and wrote down his impressions at the end of the fifteenth century was rather shocked by all this:

> The want of affection in the English is strongly manifested towards their children, for having kept them at home till they arrive at the age of seven or nine years at the utmost, they put them out, both males and females, to hard service in the houses of other people, binding them generally for another seven or nine years. And these are called apprentices, and during that time they perform all the most menial offices; and few are born who are exempted from this fate, for everyone, however rich he may be, sends away his children into the houses of others whilst he, in return, receives those of strangers into his own.*

*For the source of this extract, see the note on p. 25 above.

Left Schoolboy being beaten. 'If he has not done well, pray lash him truly' (letter from Agnes Paston, 1458). *Right* A school scene.

The answer to such accusations given by the English would correctly be not lack of love but that children might in this way learn better manners. It was an age of etiquette in which manners signified the breeding which in turn was the road to advancement: an age of ambition, more strikingly noticeable among the upper and middling classes than elsewhere. Apprentices, undergraduates and children serving in households were freely beaten.

> Pray Greenfield faithfully to send me word [wrote the formidable Agnes Paston in 1458], whom Clement Paston has to see to his duty in learning. And if he has not done well and will not truly amend, pray him to lash him truly . . . as his last master did, the best he ever had, at Cambridge. Tell Greenfield that if he will undertake to bring him to good rule and learning, and I can see him doing his duty, I will give him £6 13s. 4d. for his labour. . . . *

Nor did the idea of domestic service arouse repugnance. A boy placed in a large household was a *valet*, which meant 'young boy'. He waited at table without loss of status. The same idea persists in verbal form when the waiter in modern France is summoned as '*garçon*'. It was simply a stage in the boy's life, and in serving his apprenticeship he mixed freely with his elders. Few barriers existed between professional and private life, for the barriers were less horizontal ones between age-groups than vertical ones between social classes. 'The family was a moral and social rather than a sentimental reality,' as M. Ariès puts it, and this was equally true among the poor, whose children worked and lived in the larger environment of village, farm or great house.

The change occurred with the extension of school education. Formerly,

* *Paston Letters*, I, No. 311.

the school had played quite a minor role except for clerics. In the fifteenth century, however, an increasing number of people wanted their sons 'put to school', especially fathers who were of the gentry or yeoman class. Thomas Brampston, yeoman of Northfleet in Kent, left money in 1511 for his son 'to be founden to scole or otherwise to be ordered' before he was twenty-one;* likewise, the son of John Goodwin of Wrotham in 1495, till the boy was twenty-four.† In 1466, John Kelom, otherwise called Draper, gentleman and steward of the Abbey of Lessness in north Kent, left lands in Crayford to his sons to find them (*ad exhibendum*) to school till they were come to years of discretion. If then one of them wanted to become a priest he was to have an income for five years but no settled estate.‡ These are only three out of very many examples showing the ambitions of men on the make for their sons. Sometimes it was specified that a boy should stay at school till he could write and read English,§ and the father's will often contained menaces against children who would not follow his last rulings. The permissiveness of William Roger in 1475 was rare: each of his three children was to have £13 6*s.* 8*d.* 'to fynde thaim to the scole durynge the somme of the said money, [and] if any of thaim woll leve the scole and . . . go to othere occupacion' he was to have the unspent residue. ‖ Of course, 'school' might mean Oxford or Cambridge, just as some modern Americans refer to 'school' when an Englishman would say 'college', but it was also possible to get a business training at Oxford. The standard of attainment — English literacy — was frequently set low, and the boys in question were generally not intended to become clergy.

In such a way, English literacy was spreading. To cite one example, in 1466 twenty witnesses were examined in connection with Sir John Fastolf's will, and of these, eight and probably nine were described as literate. The average age of the men who could read was thirty-five, and they included two merchants, a mariner, a tailor and two men of husbandry (*agricultores*), all from East Anglia and most of them men who had moved their place of residence every few years.¶ Perhaps 30 per cent of the population could read in the fifteenth century and about 40 per cent by 1530, though rather fewer could also write. Nor was it narrowly a question of status or sex. In 1468 Sir John Paston was 'proud' that one of his women correspondents could read

*Somerset House, will register 'Fetiplace', folio 2.
†Somerset House, will register 'Vox', folios 29 and 34.
‡ Rochester Diocesan Will Book (in Maidstone Archive Office), vol. IV, fo. 221b, 222a.
§ ibid., VII, fo. 156 (John Chown of Shipbourne, Kent, 1514).
‖ Somerset House, will register 'Wattys', folios 172–3.
¶ *Paston Letters*, II, No. 550.

English,* and the whole correspondence is ample evidence of the literacy of women, shaky though it might sometimes be. But the drive towards literacy was predominantly a middle- and upper-class matter. The Tudor age would show more openly a new attitude towards the gentleman educated to take his place in the commonwealth of society and government, especially in a work like Sir Thomas Elyot's *Book of the Governor*. Later still, the rich would make their Grand Tour of Europe to 'finish off' their education while the working classes continued with apprenticeship.

Parallel with this ran the rise of the family, concerned with its domestic rather than lineal being, more turned in on itself, more private, less casually sociable and, above all, more interested in its children for their own sake. It was Erasmus, in his *Christian Marriage*, who propounded the modern idea that children united the family and that their physical resemblance to the parents produced affectionate feelings of intimate belonging and responsibility. Basically, domestic family life, education and interest in children for themselves and not just as rather small grown-ups, had middle-class origins and was beginning in the fifteenth century.

If the close conjugal family was on the way, it had not yet in the later Middle Ages ousted the family as an institution which stretched across the generations, attracting a deep emotional loyalty that was dynastic rather than personal. Lineal families were kept together by inheritance laws and customs. This mental attitude is expressed in literature by the use of the last will and testament as a literary device. Langland does it when he makes Piers turn to his wife and children, saying that as he is now old and grey and has enough to live on he will go and do penance on pilgrimage, so before he goes he will write his will.† And the will follows, in set terms: 'In the name of God Amen. I, Piers, make this will myself . . .,' and so on, as he leaves his soul to God, his mortal remains to the Church, and his wife shall have what he has earned by honest toil, sharing it among his children. François Villon also does it, and in fact his two greatest poems, brilliant and blistering comments on fifteenth-century Paris, are entitled *The Legacy* and *The Testament*.

In the practical order, the family's inheritance was dealt with differently in respect of moveable possessions and real, or landed, property. The former were disposed of in the testament which was proved (generally) by a church court, and no more need be said of it here. The inheritance proper descended according to the secular law or custom of the land. This has been partly dis-

---

Paston Letters, II, No. 588.
† B Text Passus VI, lines 85–107.

cussed already in Chapter 4, but a little more about it should be said here.

The main inheritance could be to the eldest son, or at least to one son, or it could be shared between the surviving children. We have already seen how in southern France the movement towards primogeniture gathered force in the course of the Middle Ages as a means of reuniting fragmented families, and how, conversely, English practice was becoming more flexible among the knightly classes and allowing them to dispose of their landed property more according to the will of the father, even if it meant bigger shares for younger sons. There was always this tension between sharing or not sharing, for each had its own desirable result. As early as the twelfth century, a moralist* had made strong points in favour of equality, and his piece, translated here, contains other matters of interest:

Let men learn to love their children from the example and from the sense of duty of crows. They diligently follow their sons as an escort when they fly and, fearing that the babies might possibly pine away, food is laid in, and they do not neglect this chore of feeding for a long time.

Now, on the other hand, the women of our own race quickly wean even those whom they love, and if they are of the richer classes they actually scorn to suckle them. If they are of the poorer classes they reject their offspring, and these are exposed and they refuse to acknowledge the ones which are found. What is more, the rich ones kill their own children in the belly, so that the inheritance may not be divided among many, and with murdering medicines they destroy the tokens of the unborn baby in the fruitful womb. Life is destroyed before it is delivered.

Who but man has preached the abandoning of children? Who but he has devised such harsh customs for fathers? Who made brothers unequal among the fraternal relationships of nature?

Our sons have to yield their place to the isolated fortune of a single rich one. The first of them is overwhelmed with the whole paternal inheritance: the second deplores the exhaustion of a rich patrimony and laments his penniless dower. But did not nature divide equally among sons? Natures assigns equally to all. . . .

This should teach you people not to make unequal in their patrimony those whom you have made equal by the title of brotherhood, and whom, indeed, you have made to be both alike by the accident of birth. You ought not to grudge their having in common a thing to which they are common heirs.

Whatever we may think of the anthropology and historical understanding of the author, he was remarkably in advance of his time by the standard of feudal England. During the period covered by this book, the partition of a

---

* This extract comes from a Latin prose bestiary which was copied in the twelfth century and is now Cambridge University Library MS. II, 4, 26. It was edited for the Roxburghe Club by M. R. James in 1928. A translation under the title *The Book of Beasts* was made by T. H. White (Cape, 1954). On p. 142 of this translation occur the words above, and I owe the reference to the kindness of Mr C. S. R. Russell.

family's inheritance among the children had, as we have seen, become possible by the device of 'enfeoffments to use' when the family held in feudal tenure. The fifteenth century was a great age for lawyers, and their ingenuity was constantly exercised in finding new ways of getting round old rules. Another good example is in the breaking of entails. An entailed estate was one which according to the common law had to descend intact down the line, usually to the eldest male heir. Sometimes this could be a nuisance, especially in a society which was paying more regard to the immediate wishes of the living, and a method of breaking the entail was thought out which was so ingenious and so typical of the time that it has an intellectual beauty and is worth explaining, stripped, it is hoped, of technical jargon but maintaining a general accuracy. It was done by a collusive lawsuit called the 'common recovery'. Suppose that Thomas is in possession of an entailed estate and wishes to free it. He will get Richard to sue him on the (pretended) excuse that the freehold is really Richard's. Thomas does not defend his right but swears that a third person, say Harold, was formerly the freeholder of the estate, and that if Harold's sale to Thomas of the estate had been illegal or irregular, he would have to compensate Thomas with lands of equal value. Harold comes along and acknowledges that this is true. Richard then asks the court's leave to have a private discussion with Harold about the legality of the original estate to Thomas. At this point Harold 'disappears' and is therefore in contempt of court, so that judgement is given against him. In other words, the court has to say that Harold had no right to make the original sale, and that the estate must be awarded to Richard in 'fee simple', which means he can do what he likes with it. Consequently, Thomas or his heirs become entitled to compensation from Harold, because it was his fault that Richard had succeeded in getting the estate. All that was then left to do was for the parties to agree privately. Richard could keep the estate if that had been the original idea, paying Thomas a market price for it; or Richard could sell it to anyone Thomas designated. In short, the entail had been broken, and the estate had become a marketable commodity again. Needless to say, the whole business was pre-arranged, and as time went on the entire transaction could be done in a lawyer's office, in writing. The third figure, the defaulting Harold, did not even need to exist.

This new flexibility in handling land, breaking down ancient feudal law and custom, did not mean that elder sons were losing their favoured position, because the feeling that they had a special claim to the bulk of the inheritance persisted, especially among families of considerable property. There was still a strong primogenitary sense. Over and above this, though, there was also a strong sense that a family should stick together, and that if any member had to sell land to raise cash, he ought to let a kinsman have first refusal. About 1452, Agnes wrote to John Paston saying

> ... Sir John Fastolf has sold Hellesden to Boleyn of London, and if it be so, it seems he will sell more. Wherefore, I pray you, as you will have my love and blessing, that you will help and do your duty that something were purchased for your two brothers. I suppose Sir John Fastolf, if he were spoken to, would be glad to let his kinsmen have part than strange men. . . . *

Again, in 1460, a Kentishman called John Ketyll left directions in his testament that none of his sons should sell any part of the inheritance, which was going to be divided among them (in Kentish fashion) to anyone else except one of themselves.† The sentiment seems natural enough in a landed, kin-conscious society, and can be matched by similar arrangements in France. Even in southern France, home of individualism, the kinsmen's right of first refusal, called 'le retrait lignager', became statutory in 1469.

To belong to a family, or at least to a substantial household, was in the Middle Ages a guarantee of one's respectability and answerability before the law. Mere villagers had to be organized in 'tithings' or local groups which would be answerable for their trespasses in the manorial court. But it was better to belong to the household of a great man. When law and order became weak at certain moments in the late Middle Ages because the central government was weak, it was more than ever necessary to have a 'good lord' who would look after you and support you if you were in trouble. This could be abused. A malefactor might run off to a powerful lord and get him to inter-fere with the processes of justice in return for some kind of service or adherence. This was called 'maintenance': the great man maintained the wrongdoer against the law, and he could do this because he had all the physical force and moral support of a powerful and possibly uniformed household behind him.

But even from remote times, the man who had no lord at all, no 'fixed address', had been suspect, and he has remained so, through the fifteenth century and up to the present day. In later medieval England, wanderers were suspicious characters unless they could account properly for their wandering by assuming the appearance of pilgrims or clergy, merchants or accredited messengers. In particular, sailors and friars, professional travellers often loosely tied to a settled abode, were by many considered to be somewhat un-

* *Paston Letters*, I, No. 183.
† Rochester Will Book, vol. II, folio 178.

desirable. They could be useful as messengers, but also as spies. The Lancastrian secret service employed them: 'the Duke of Somerset has spies going into every lord's house of the land', wrote a Paston correspondent in 1454, just before the civil wars broke out. 'Some go as friars, some as shipmen taken on the sea . . . who report to him all they can see or hear about the Duke of York. Therefore make good watch and beware of such spies.' * The same year an information was laid against one Robert Ledham for riotous behaviour, and the accusers said he kept a lot of misgoverned characters about him, 'to whom he gives clothing, and he gives also to other men who do not dwell in his household; and of the twenty men in question not more than eight are occupied in husbandry'. † The Pastons' canny chaplain and agent, James Gloys, remarked that in a certain lawsuit he had been offered sureties, but he 'would have no shipmen, who possessed nothing and were men who did not care once they were at sea whether they came back again or not'.‡

Households of every grade and size were the organs of society within which men, women and children dwelt and enjoyed their being according to their degree and vocation. Yet every household had its links with others and with the outside world. These connections were both political and personal, but the dividing-line between social intercourse and the governance of the realm is an impossible one to draw in the Middle Ages. The intensely personal character of politics has often been pointed out. Great earls and barons, surrounded and followed by numerous retinues, expected close relationships with the king, and were expected in return to attend upon him when summoned. To stay away from court at such a moment was a dangerous sign of hostility. How easily the sulking of a baron was construed as the whisper of disaffection or the prelude to the gathering of forces! 'The Duke of Suffolk is able to keep daily in his house more men than Daubeny has hairs on his head,'§ remarked a correspondent in 1465; and it required only an order and the scurrying of messengers to bring sworn retainers in from the countryside. Conversely, if the king lost his temper, or stayed glowering away from parliament, favouring his friends excessively or sheltered behind an impenetrable screen of courtiers, then the country experienced a political crisis. In times of peace, too, free from 'rumours and flying tales', ‖ when good will prevailed, the political and administrative life of the country breathed

* *Paston Letters*, I, No. 195.
† ibid., No. 201.
‡ ibid., No. 146.
§ ibid., II, No. 502 (1465).
‖ ibid., III, Nos. 723, 724.

through the movement of magnates and their households. Bishops or their deputies moved constantly about their dioceses, to confirm children, ordain clerks, bless and consecrate or to enjoy a fresh scene and keep useful contact with all manner of people. King and baron itinerated and expected men of the locality to come to them. Thus were they seen, their power felt through their physical presence, the interest of all quickened by hearsay, a glimpse of the great man, or a hearing of some difficult case before the mobile court. It was social life too: to be summoned for a coronation or an enthronement, a tournament or theatricals, these were the moments when 'fellowships' met, drank, talked and did business. A worldly gaiety prevailed in Lambeth Palace when Archbishop Morton's household produced *Fulgens and Lucrece* for its Christmas dramatics, written by one of his chaplains, and the earliest known secular play in England. Sir John Paston, the family's greatest socialite, complained with a mild satisfaction in 1476 that 'my hand was hurt at the tourney at Waltham last Wednesday. I wish you had been there and seen it, for it was the goodliest sight that was seen in England these forty years. . . .'*

Even though a large household might consist of servants and retainers, menacing or quiescent, the family of kindred and affinity still remained as the tissue of politics and society, sundered though it may have been by distance or immediate political loyalties or sharp variations in wealth itself. Men could quarrel bitterly with their kinsmen. At worst this meant civil war — 'the escalation of private feuds' — as when the Nevilles divided in anger over their vast inheritance and its partition between the children of Ralph's

Paston Letters, II, No. 572.

A knight being armed for combat, at the time of Sir John Paston. Late fifteenth century.

successive wives. On a smaller canvas, William Paston was anxious to disclaim a ne'er-do-well in 1425 who claimed to be his cousin: 'I have many poor men of my kin, but one so false was never of my kin.' * For all that, it was natural for men to support their kinsmen if they could. When Lord Scales wrote in 1459 to the Duke of Norfolk's council, he said:

> my lord of Norfolk pretendeth title to certain lands of Sir John Paston's. . . . And forasmuch as marriage is fully concluded betwixt the said Sir John Paston and one of my nearest kinswomen, I doubt not that your reason well conceiveth that nature must compel me the rather to show my good will, assistance and favour unto the said Sir John in such things as concern his inheritance.

Though he himself was a member of the duke's council, yet 'I heartily pray you . . . to advise my lord that all entries, felling of woods and distraining of tenants . . . be ceased.'†

Favour and patronage to kinsmen is visible on every hand, whether a plea to use influence at court to get a son a local controllership of customs,‡ or whether a new archbishop like Warham bestowed good leases of parks and arables and mills upon a galaxy of relatives.

The extension of family feeling was felt by its members across the boundaries of space and time. Families proliferated and spread. The girls married and went away; the boys made careers in law or business or the church. But such correspondence as we have suggests not merely the business arrangements of grasping and mercenary people, but an eagerness for letters and news from distant members every bit as ardent as that displayed among Victorian families. Not infrequently, the central recipient and passer-on of news was the mother or one of the older women. So often these are the keepers of the tribal memory, sensitive to kinship, treasuring letters like albums of faded snapshots. They worried at silence.

> . . . I pray you let my grandam and my cousin Clare have knowledge how that I desired you to let them have knowledge of the tidings in this letter [wrote John Paston in 1462]. I pray you [he continued] let my mother have knowledge how that I and my fellowship and your servants are at the writing of this letter in good health, blessed be God. I pray you let my father have knowledge of this letter and of the other letter I sent to my mother by Felbridge's man; and how that I pray both him and my mother lowly of their blessings. I pray you that you will send me some letter how you do, and of your tidings with you, for I think long that I hear no word from my mother and you. I pray you that this bill may recommend me to my sister Margery and to my mistress

* *Paston Letters*, i, No. 5.
†ibid., ii, No. 603.
‡ibid., No. 456.

Joan Gayne, and to all good masters and fellows within Caister. I sent no letter to my
father, never since I departed from you, for I could get no man to London, and never
since. I pray you let Richard Calle see this letter.*

The litany gathers up the wishes of a medieval heart, anxious for communion with the reality it knew best and desired with sharpest longing: the
family and its household.

There were, of course, no postmen, and men endured the distractions of
irregularity and the barrier of distances which now seem slight. If money
were available a man could be hired specially, or at least a traveller could be
paid to slip another letter into his pouch, folded and sealed with wax. 'The
Treasurer's name is Sir John Fog, but he is not in London nor with the king,
so I can not have the letter sent him unless I hire a man to bear it.' † 'I send
you a letter enclosed herein from my nephew,' and on the back of this one is
written, 'the man would not take my letter unless I was willing to give him
2*d.* for the bearing'.

The extension of family feeling over time must be emphasized with equal
strength, though the argument is a little more elaborate. It has been explained
already that in the fifteenth century the notion of the conjugal family in the
very present, oriented round the domestic circle and the children, was only
just beginning, and that men thought dynastically of the line which stretched
backwards and forwards across the generations. Such lineal ambitions were
expressed through the laws of inheritance, complex beyond belief with their
entails and wills and cross-remainders, suited to a world uncushioned by social
security organized by government, unfragmented by industrial wage-earning
and insouciant permissiveness towards the young. In a sense, too, the idea of
inheritance possessed a reverse application. As will be seen more fully in
Chapter 8, all the obits and Masses and divine services for the dead signified
an anxiety for dead parents and forbears, that their spiritual estate should be
safeguarded, that their repose in the fires of Purgatory should be brief, and
that they should enjoy the happiness of heaven by such earthly works as the
Church prescribed. To die without making a will was almost as bad as to die
unconfessed. To make a will without thought for intercessory prayer was near
to heresy. It did occasionally happen at the very end of the Middle Ages
among people who are not otherwise known to have held heretical views.
John Shelley, gentleman of Bexley in Kent, left the residue of his goods and
chattels to his son William to his own use, to dispose of them as he pleased

* *Paston Letters,* II, No. 465.
† ibid., No. 540 (1466).

'for the health of the soul of the testator and all Christian souls, and not if it does not please him'.* But such indifference was rare. The endowment of services or chantries was usual, and middle-class as well as aristocratic. These institutions flourished in order to send heavenwards a flow of intercession for the dead, for benefactors and friends and, always, father and mother. 'John Huberd is to keep a yearly obit in Shoreham church of 6*d., so long as the world standeth,'* wrote Nicholas Huberd in his will of 1496.† From the secular viewpoint, a vast drain was in this way made upon the saved resources of propertied families, nourishing a clerical industry upon which all too soon a new and impatient world was to exact a complete revenge. This will be said again, but in this chapter the context is familial and not religious. People set aside property for a purpose that was a family one, in such a way that the term 'reverse inheritance' may not unjustly be coined for it since it benefited, or was held to benefit, those of the family whose lives were over instead of those who were yet to come.

> Time present and time past
> Are both perhaps present in time future,
> And time future contained in time past.‡

Even medieval critics bear a testimony to this effect, as when Wyclif castigated the chantry system for giving the opportunity to men for the vain perpetuation in the world of family names.

Perhaps in this case the point may be finally made with a more touching sympathy by allusion not to England but to southern France, where the heir of one who had died without making a will might none the less make pious provision for the deceased. The Abbey of St Gilles in Languedoc, scene of pilgrimages from north and south, had a veritable business by which men of all ranks might 'ordain' prayers for the souls of the dead. Such a one was the labourer, Grégoire Espérandieu, who in 1524 made a gift for the soul of his dead wife, 'who during her whole life lived honestly and chastely and was a hard-working and virtuous woman, looking after their common property with every care'. And this he did for the salvation of the soul of her 'who during married life performed so many, so pleasing, untellable and free services for him'.§

*Somerset House, will register 'Hogan', folio 5 (1531).
†Somerset House, will register 'Vox', folio 28.
‡T. S. Eliot, 'Burnt Norton', lines 1—3.
§Text in R. Aubenas, 'L'*ordinatio pro anima* en Languedoc au XVe–XVIe siècles', *Revue d'histoire de l'église de France*, XXIX (1943), pp. 257—62.

7 Attitudes Towards Authority

This is a difficult chapter to write. It is not a political or constitutional sketch about the authorities of earth and heaven in later medieval England: King, Council, Parliament, Church. There are books in plenty about these. It is about attitudes. Whom did men respect and fear? What did the neighbours say? 'To whom, then,' as a famous question once ran, 'shall we go?'

In all conscience such answers are hard enough to come by today, when the social pressures of Camberley or Burnley or London may be so various and their discovery so much a matter of intuition, arrived at by long residence, differing from person to person, or changing with the changing years. How dangerous, even deplorable, for a historian with any pretensions to scholarly self-respect to venture upon such a field in an age as remote as the fifteenth century! Yet why should the attempt not be made, even at the cost of the reader's scepticism or of rapid obsolescence? Some sort of starting-point may be made by suggesting as a modern parallel that Englishmen today on the whole respect, shall we say, their judiciary, their medical profession, their monarchy, sportsmen, airmen, and firemen, whereas more of them are indifferent or hostile towards the politicians and the priests.

For the fifteenth century the scene is complicated by class divisions which, for all their mobility, are sharper than in the more homogeneous industrial society of today. But, as we have seen, England was then a self-consciously aristocratic society in which men emulated, or thought that they emulated, the great lords whose houses dotted the land and whose retinues commanded it within wide radiuses of influence. So it is fitting to begin with an aristocrat, and to read the well-known letter written by the Duke of Suffolk on the eve of his murder, as he set down on paper a sort of hierarchy of pieties which ring truer than mere conventional noises.* In April 1450 he wrote to his son

*Paston Letters, I, No. 91.

Plate 7. Fortune with her wheel. 'Fortune, which that permutacioun of thinges hath. . .'

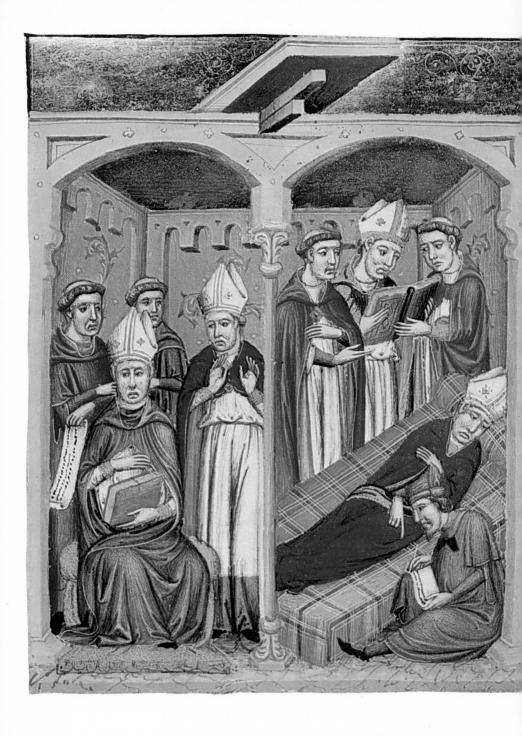

a farewell in which he enjoined him to be faithful to his Maker and sorry for his faults, and continued

> ...next Him, above all earthly kings, to be true liege man in heart, in will, in thought, in deed, unto the king our most high and dread sovereign lord, to whom you and I have been so much bound to, charging you as a father can and may rather to die than to be the contrary. Thirdly, I charge you, my dear son, to love and worship your lady and mother, obey her commandments and believe her counsel and advice which, never fear, will be the best and truest for you. ...

So, among earthly authorities, he preferred above all others the king. There is no surprise here, even though Suffolk had special reason for gratitude to the person of Henry VI, who to many others was in himself scarcely dread sovereign or lord. Reverence for the king and a sense of his indispensability was wellnigh universal, even among rebels who would break an archbishop's crockery and smite off his head, or curse the pope, disdaining his evident powers to damn 'which would not hurt a fly'.

The fifteenth-century king was a practical ruler, not merely a well-dressed symbol of unity or paragon of domestic bliss. Much depended on his very presence, which men might approach for the redress of grievances or the begging of some favour, and it has been convincingly argued that the deposition of Henry VI was much less a failure of loyalty to the monarchy or a dynasty than a failure on Henry's part to remain accessible to the generality of political men.

There was in the king a curious mixture of remoteness and vital presence. Richard II both imposed himself and removed his presence when he wished, without tact. The palace revolution of 1399 which replaced Richard by Henry of Lancaster substituted for one dynasty another which seemed to promise some freedom from gross imposition but scarcely replaced a remote and auto-cratic monarchy with an informal and popular one. To have done this would have been wholly out of character with the times. True enough, Henry IV promised with some glibness 'to be counselled and governed by the honour-able, wise and discreet persons of his realm', and this was a true and suitable gesture of acknowledgement that lords and now the parliamentary Commons had a right to give advice and to suggest control of the money they provided. But he and his counsellors were strongly conscious that everyone 'ought to be led and governed in his estate and degree',* and displayed a poor opinion of the pride of the common people. In fact, the Lancastrian monarchy in its turn (1399–1461) tended to become increasingly remote, not only from the

---

Rotuli Parliamentorum (Record Commission, 1783–1832), III, p. 415.

Plate 8. A bishop dictates his will

Coronation of a king, painted *c.* 1382.

common people, but from whole sections of the nobility and gentry who, from the 1440s, were screened away from the royal presence by court friends and curialist ministers. It was this as much as anything that broke the dynasty, since the king in effect had not only to be an ark of the covenant but available to men thirsty for private favour and needing at least his ear for their supplications and confidences. The king was king, fount of justice, and none was higher than he in the practical life of the day. For him to fail or become enfeebled dried up confidence and with it financial credit, so that he could neither borrow on the security of taxes he could not raise, nor repay the debts he had already incurred. Such a failure left no alternative at first but the devolution of power into private hands, and, ultimately, his replacement by a king who could enrich himself by massive confiscations and once more make himself available to men to whom he could grant something, able by the very fact to express in power his wishes and will. When the Duke of York in 1460 attempted to claim the throne, laying his

130

hand upon it and saying that he knew of none who should not come to him rather than he to approach another in reverence, the surrounding lords stood amazed and discomforted; and the Archbishop slipped out to explain to Henry VI in a near-by room what was happening. But the civil war and the escape of Henry with his redoubtable French Queen left no more to do than to replace him, for he had gone inaccessibly into the remote north.

Such an attitude towards royal authority could not be changed in a royalist society. But a psychological change occurred when Edward IV, son of Richard of York, replaced Henry in 1461. Acclaimed by a small party of supporters, he was favoured by the judgement of battle, and his possession of the throne swayed men to his side by the fact of success itself. Authority derives from power. Edward was very young, personable, and a leader. He could make himself felt. In some way he and his father had appealed in the 1450s to the lesser people of the kingdom, perhaps by skilful propaganda and subversion, perhaps by contrast with the courtiers and bishops surrounding Henry VI who seemed like a wall of self-sufficiency, military ineptitude against the ancient enemy of France, and private greed. At all events, Edward IV could make himself felt. If he was a womanizer who incurs the censure of later times, we are also told he married Elizabeth Woodville 'because he had long loved her', and a wilful and worldly heart lay beneath the handsome and ruthless exterior. *'Beau prince entre les beaux du monde,'* noted Philippe Commynes, the French reporter. Professor Lander has well said, 'Edward never risked the contempt which his solitary, shabby blue velvet gown had brought upon Henry VI.' Edward's magnificence was a weapon of politics, and his badge of the sun in splendour shone the more effectively because his acts and his character enabled him to pay his bills promptly. Another observer, Dominic Mancini, wrote of Edward's easiness of access, geniality towards those whom he overawed, yet his capacity to appear terrible in season. He conveyed in a new and successful manner the twin attributes of remoteness and availability. He was remote in this organized splendour, laying emphasis upon his secular enthronement in Westminster Hall on the marble throne — the 'King's Bench' — acclaimed by lords and by-standers as he wore his cap of estate, and only then consenting to follow the monks of Westminster across the road for his sacring. He was also often geographically remote, out of necessity, as he journeyed the country to bring order and settle troubles in company with his judges. He meant to be obeyed. In October 1461, half a year after his seizure of power, Clement Paston wrote that ' . . . the king said, "we have sent two privy seals to Paston by two yeomen of our chamber, and he disobeys them; but we will send him another to-

A messenger to the king. Late four-teenth-century France.

morrow and, by God's mercy, if he come not he shall die for it. We will make all other men beware by him how they shall disobey our writing."'*

Government and political life operated through getting the king's ear, seeking him out, trying to persuade him, interceding through those who stood near him: 'labouring him', as the phrase went. 'I have laboured daily my lord of Essex, Treasurer of England, to have moved the king [about the manor of Dedham] ... every morning before he went to the king, and oftentimes enquired of him if he had moved the king in these matters.'†

For his part, the king needed tact and discretion, not despotic whim. The great lords were still powers in the land. On one occasion, when buttonholed and asked to do something the Duke of Norfolk would not have liked, Edward simply turned away without a definite answer and talked to some-body else. The parliamentary Commons, too, less great than the nobility as they were, had none the less to be handled carefully by the king. Petitions were already being addressed to them as 'the right wise, honourable and discreet Commons', and their assent had become necessary to the authority of parliamentary acts.

Right worshipful sir [wrote John Berney to John Paston in July 1461], I pray you heartily to labour for that the king may write to me, giving me thanking of the good will and service that I have done unto him, and in being with him against his adversaries and rebellions, as well in the north as in this country of Norfolk, and in that the king should please the commons of this country. For they grudge, and say how that the king receiveth such of this country, etc., as have been his great enemies, and oppressors of the commons, and such as have assisted his Highness be not rewarded; and it is to be considered, or else it will hurt,

*Paston Letters, II, No. 417.
†ibid., No. 410: John Paston to his father (August 1461).

as me seemeth by reason. And in aid of this changeable rule it were necessary to move the good lords, spiritual and temporal, by the which that might be reformed.*

The 'good lords spiritual and temporal': the phrase introduces that cluster of authorities under which the life of England, political and social, was most closely run. Let it be repeated: for all the social mobility among gentry, merchants, yeomen and peasants, England was still an aristocratic country. Men and women admired lords, feared them, and aped what they took to be their manners and mode of life. The nobility set the tone, even while they changed it. There was no professional intelligentsia, as in the modern world, actively to decry the noble norm and offer a substitute. To this extent the pageantry of the Shakespearian stage is not wholly a world of play-wright's myth, but reproduced what was still true when Shakespeare wrote, and would remain true until the Dukes of Omnium shrank back into their twentieth-century islands of clubland and country house. Lordship ful-filled a function in public and private life which is hard to re-create in the imagination at this moment. Through the power of the local lord men

---

* *Paston Letters*, II, No. 404.

Richard Beauchamp, Earl of Warwick, being made Lieut-enant-General and Governor of both France and Normandy by Henry VI, 16 July 1437. Political power was still wielded most effectively by the great lords.

were protected, advanced or destroyed. The hackneyed phrase of the letter-writer who signed himself 'Nameless atte this tyme' in 1450 must be repeated: ' . . . spend somewhat of your goods now and get you good lordship and friendship, for on that hang all the law and the prophets (*quia ibi pendet tota lex et prophetae*).'* To Sir John Fastolf, too, in a tricky moment, the Archbishop of Canterbury was 'the lord earthly I have most trust on'.†

This is not, I think, a specifically *later* medieval situation, but in the fifteenth century the power and opinions of lords seem at moments especially strong, partly because we happen to have the personal, intimate letters that tell us about it, and partly because the overriding authority of the king and his judicial advisers hung often in doubt. Lords did not spend much time in posturing like male models. Great and small, they recruited followers about them, 'affinities', men with arms who knew how to use them for local and temporary security in days that were evil and times that were graphically described as 'right wild'. Margaret Paston in 1465 was doing her best to protect the property of her husband John against invaders of it who had the Duke of Suffolk behind them.

> . . . And Piers Waryn, otherwise called Piers at Sloth, which is a flickering fellow and a busy with a master Philip and the bailiff of Cossey, he had a plough going in your land at Drayton, and your servants took his plough. Next morning master Philip and the bailiff of Cossey came with a great number of people, that is, 160 men and more in harness, and it will never lie in your power to foil them. . . . ‡

Thus, in their smaller way, country gentry like the Pastons had to resort to such means themselves, for they too in a rural sense were lords of men and lands upon whom relied others who gathered in force about them.

> I have hired at wages to help you and Daubeney keep the place at Caister four well-assured and true men to do all manner of things they be desired to do in safeguarding the place; and moreover they be proved men and cunning [skilful] in war and feats of arms, and they can well shoot both guns and crossbows, and mend and string them, and devise bulwarks . . . and they will, as need is, keep watch and ward. They be sad [serious] and well-advised men, save one of them, who is bald, and called William Peny, who is as good a man as goeth on earth saving a little he will, as I understand, be a little *copschotyn* [trigger happy?], but yet he is no brawler.§

*Paston Letters, I, No. 116.
†ibid., No. 227.
‡ibid., II, No. 502.
§ibid., No. 592.

The social and political truth is that power and influence were balanced according to the lie of forces like this. The 'constitutional' truth is that men were bound together in affinities, retinues, or even temporary wage-contracts, by means of agreements which, when written in legal form, were called indentures, and which promised service in peace and/or war to the lord, against all manner of comers, occasionally not even excepting the king. The psychology behind such relationships may be glimpsed through the very style and words by which men addressed each other in their written communications. The gentle phrases of modern letters between men of Cabinet rank — 'my dear Bill' — which may conceal a whole spectrum of friendship or menace behind an artless informality, had no place in a world of acknowledged degree and order. The stylization was more formal, yet it betrayed inner attitudes more readily. To a very great man, like the Earl of Oxford, one would write, 'Right high and mighty prince and my right good lord, I recommend me unto your good lordship.'* To an inferior, king or lord would use some such formula as 'Right trusty and entirely well beloved' — words redolent of the trust and loyalty they so ardently hoped for in a society that was deeply unsure of such qualities, much as a visitor to a strange house might confront the suspicious house-dog with encouraging cries of 'Good dog, good dog'. Even King Edward IV was at pains to underline the security he needed by thanking the Commons in his first parliament thus:

James Strangeways [Speaker] and you who have come for the commons of this my land, I thank you as heartily as I can for the *true hearts* and tender considerations which you have had for my right and title ... and now, thanks be to Almighty God by whose grace all victory springs, and thanks to your *true hearts* and great assistance, I have been restored to what is mine by right and title. For this also I thank you, and for the tender and *true hearts* which you have shown me by having tenderly in remembrance the correction of the horrible murder and cruel death of the lord my father, of my brother Rutland, and of my cousin Salisbury. . . . And for the *faithful and loving hearts* ... I thank you with all my heart. And if I had any better possession with which to reward you than my body, you should have it. Which body will always be ready for your defence, never sparing nor ceasing from any danger. I pray you all, for your hearty assistance and good continuance, as I shall be unto you your very righteous and loving liege lord.†

To this hierarchy of attitudes, towards God, king and mother, set out in Suffolk's letter at the beginning of this chapter, something has now already been explained about the king and parents, something will shortly be added

* *Paston Letters*, I, No. 106.
† *Rotuli Parliamentorum*, v, 487 (my italics).

Left 'Traylebaston': English thugs with offensive weapons. A fourteenth-century drawing. *Right* Parliament at Westminster, *c.* 1400.

about attitudes towards God and his church, and something has been interjected about the lords, related to the king and attentive upon him, but capable, at moments of political fragmentation, of taking upon themselves the local attributes of kingship itself.

This must be emphasized by saying that the local lord was for the mass of country people most of the time truly in a regal position, and this lordship was expressed most obviously in the local judicial and manorial courts in private hands with which the country was still littered. Men of small account who could not pay fines to be quit of the obligation were summoned usually at regular intervals through the year to attend the courts of lordships: at three-weekly intervals for minor matters, six-monthly for matters of petty criminal jurisdiction. Such tenants came in response to public criers, knocks on the door by the bedel, or by reference to the calendar that men and women kept in their heads, refreshed and oriented by the feasts of the church. Court-keeping was an onerous duty with servile undertones. But for the lord successfully to keep his court was the very hallmark of local dominance and the display of his effective authority. To the tenants it mattered much who the lord was, or when the lordship passed from one hand to another:

Right worshipful husband ... please know that I sent on Lammas Day [1 August] to Drayton Thomas Bonde and Sir James Gloys to hold the court in your name, and claim your title, for I could get none other body to keep the court or would go there except Thomas Bonde, because I suppose they were afraid of the people

136

that should be there of the Duke of Suffolk's party ... some of them having rusty pole-axes and bills, coming into the manor yard to keep the court. ...*

To enter a disputed property was very much a physical process, involving the need to stay there, receive the rents, and preside over the proceedings.

To the small people of the countryside, the lord's court fulfilled the functions which today are supplied partly by the local magistrate's court, partly by the Post Office where licences are paid for, and also partly by the more casual gatherings of neighbours where names are bandied about and good reputations (and more often ill reputations) made known in the community.

The same interested respect for judicial meetings may be observed all the way up the scale. The fifteenth century was an age of intense litigiousness, and one of which it is often, and correctly, said that the law was liable to perversion by fear of armed power or by favour of bribes. Yet this litigiousness can itself be read as a faith in legal process as such, rather than in the unorganized seizure of right by mere might.

Above the level of local and private courts resided authorities which, for all their defects, men respected. In the king's central courts of Common Bench and King's Bench, endless disputes about land were entertained, transactions registered, and the consequential title-deeds or decisions recorded, paid for and treasured. In the royal Chancery, an equitable jurisdiction attracted ever more petitioners who sought protection from violent characters or remedies which the common law courts, grown somewhat rigid in a changing world, were unable to supply — protection for estates in trust or situations which called for a sense of fair play or 'natural justice'. Royal punishment of crime could be severe and horrible when felony, punishable by hanging, was applicable to thefts of relatively small amounts. Yet the courts did not renounce the awe which they attracted through the leniency they surprisingly practised: acquittals were frequent, and felonious behaviour was often regarded as simple trespass for which a fine was payable. Judges and jurors could learn that the less they took of blood the more they took of treasure. Imprisonment itself was rare, save as a temporary measure to secure the accused pending trial or to deal with clerics who still might with luck escape the judgement of blood by reason of their clerical order.

If royal and seignorial courts were a dominant authority which commanded respect, the church courts too were a force to be reckoned with, though in a different way. They touched the lives of more people than any other tribunal save possibly the manorial courts, and they touched them in a manner which

---

*Paston Letters, II, No. 518; cf. Nos. 467, 491, 529.

then was irritating enough and today would be insufferable to contemplate. A study of the archbishop's and archdeacon's courts in the diocese of Canterbury has shown that few escaped their attention. 'An index of plaintiffs introducing suits into the courts would include all the important persons of east Kent, all the religious houses within the diocese, and many of the wealthy citizens and mayors of Canterbury and the Cinque Ports'. The defendants in cases where the church itself prosecuted were more numerous and varied still, mostly accused of crimes which nowadays would be classed as sins, or at least disposed of in quickly forgotten paragraphs of journalistic gossip columns. Not only had the church courts jurisdiction over testaments and matrimony, about which a good deal has already here been written, but they claimed and exercised cognizance over the moral behaviour of lay men and women. Proceedings for sexual offences and for debt (where the offence was technically perjury) were begun by these courts and were notified in the villages by the court's emissaries known as summoners. Chaucer has for all time drawn the summoner's sardonic cartoon and prefaced it by a description of his master the archdeacon:

> In my own district once there used to be
> A fine archdeacon, one of high degree,
> Who boldly did the execution due
> On fornication and on witchcraft too,
> Bawdry, adultery and defamation,
> Breaches of wills and contract, spoliation
> Of church endowment, failure in the rents
> And tithes and disregard of sacraments. . . . *

The summoner, or apparitor, was probably the least-loved of all the representatives of authority. He travelled about with a pouch full of citations addressed to men and women who had been delated to the court. Here is an actual example of one of these citations, dated about 1509 and referring to Cranbrook in the weald of Kent:

> Cyte a woman with child in the house of Thomas Low
> Also cite Robert Donke dwelling with John Brad
> Cite Thomas Barrow which is defamed with many women. . . .

There follow about ten more names of men, wives and widows, including

> Cite the Vicar of Benynden.†

The Friar's Tale, lines 1–8 (Transl. Nevill Coghill, Penguin Books, 1951), p. 317.
†Printed by B. L. Woodcock, *Medieval Ecclesiastical Courts in the Diocese of Canterbury* (Oxford, 1952), p. 133.

Failure to present oneself or to perform the prescribed penance was regarded as contumacy, and after forty days' contumacy the church authorities could bring the king's sheriff to their aid to arrest the accused person and hold him in durance till he repented. It is probably true to say that attitudes towards this kind of ecclesiastical jurisdiction were marked by a dislike ranging from mockery to a hatred unparalleled by any similar feelings towards the secular courts, and certainly the 1530s saw dramatic outbursts against it. The reasons are not far to seek: church courts opened windows into men's souls and private affairs in a manner no longer acceptable, if they had ever been, and their very efficiency, greatly increased since the rise of local church courts in the thirteenth century, exacerbated these feelings; and, further, the church courts appeared more than others to make distinction between persons, so that men of wealth and standing could more easily commute their humiliating penances for money, partly because they could pay, and partly because the courts thought they should spare 'worshipful' men experiences which would shame them in public. No doubt resentments of both these kinds were often mingled and confused in men's minds in an age which, for all its defects, was developing more personal notions of individual conscience, when the clatter of money was coming to be associated with the expiation of faults, and when the faults themselves were often those which normal people could no longer reckon as justiciable in a public forum.

The immense area of jurisdiction embraced by an ecclesiastical court may be seen by a glance at any subject index of such a court's Act Books: adultery, assaults on priests, delay in baptisms, blasphemy, breaking promises, feeding horses in churchyards, defamation, heretical opinions, incontinence, matrimonial offences, failure to perform penances, sabbath breaking, usury and witchcraft — to name only a selection.* The list is quite co-ordinate with Chaucer's.

This chapter may be ended by choosing some observations on witchcraft and sorcery, for these offences were becoming more frequent and, more exactly to the point, they cast an oblique but strong light upon the attitudes of the day. This is arguable for the very reason that sorcery was (in the writer's view) objectively nonsense. If someone commits a crime like murder or theft, there is no more to be learned, except the platitude that murder and theft were more or less common crimes. If, however, considerable numbers of people in a city like London consulted sorcerers, we may expect to learn more about what such people in their hearts desired

*Hale, *Precedents*, Index.

or feared. On this assumption, it would appear that in the late Middle Ages three of the commonest reasons for recourse to sorcerers were the wish to cause death or injury to enemies, especially political enemies, the desire to recover stolen property, and the wish for success in love or matrimony.

The political offence of treason has always attracted penalties of extreme cruelty, but never more so than in an era like the later Middle Ages when political order was unstable. At this time, men were especially prone to project their fears on to supposed witches. In the well-known case of Eleanor Cobham in 1441, the accusation was that this luckless woman (why was it so often an accusation against women?) had compassed the king's death by means of black magic. Two men, said to be learned in these arts, had been consulted: Roger Bultybroke and Thomas Southwell, a canon of St Stephen's, Westminster, which was a collegiate foundation closely associated with the royal family. By using special books, images of the king's likeness, swords, circular objects, and by performing black masses in the name of the Holy Trinity, St Mary, and the Holy Ghost they had hoped to bring the king to his death through 'despair'.*

On a lower political level, there are cases where sorcerers thought to destroy an enemy by making his image in wax and then consuming it with fire like a candle, in the belief that the victim would die.

London diocesan court also dealt with many cases where poor people went to magicians in order to recover lost or stolen property. In 1476 Nazareth Jarbrey of Totell Street, Westminster, approached Thomas Barley. After offering certain prayers, Barley gazed into a beryl stone and claimed to see a man who reported that a pyx set with pearls and precious stones had been stolen from the house of the client's mother. At another time, at the suggestion of a clerk, Nazareth again went to Thomas Barley's house and divined two supposed thieves whose names he did not know but who could be identified by their clothing and personal appearance. Again, in 1509, a woman consulted a sorcerer in Charterhouse Lane. When he looked into a mirror he saw one Christopher Sandon observing how Alice Ancetyr hid a precious rosary in the straw of her bed, and then creeping in and stealing it. Cases like this must have been founded upon previous suspicion, and were sometimes judged in the church court not as sorcery or theft but as a defamation of the individual accused. To this extent the courts were protecting the rules of evidence.

Affairs of the heart occupied an even more pre-eminent place in the

*An English Chronicle, edited by J. S. Davies (Camden Society, 1856), p. 57. The other cases are drawn from Hale's Precedents, pp. 43, 123, 284.

sorcerer's repertoire. Joan Beverley, a married woman, employed witchcraft in 1482 to make Robert Stanton and another gentleman of Gray's Inn love her and none other; the result was a fight between the two and the flight of the husband, and the woman was accused of being a whore. The court must be praised again for being extremely down to earth in these matters. Sadder and more illuminating of the social scene is the story of the widow Margaret Geffrey who between 1480 and 1492 fell victim to a cruel confidence trick. The deposition of witnesses has preserved the case in dialogue form:

RICHARD
LANKISTON: Thou art a poor widow, and it were alms to help thee to a marriage, and if thou wilt do any cost in spending any money, thou shalt have a man worth £1,000.

MARGARET
GEFFREY: How may that be?

R.L.: My wife knoweth a cunning man that by his cunning can cause a woman to have any man that she hath favour to, and that shall be upon your warranties. For she hath put it in execution aforetime. And this shall cost money.

M.G.: I have no goods save two mazers [goblets] to support me, my mother and my children, and if they were sold and I fail in my purpose I, my mother and my children were undone.

R.L.: Deliver me the mazers, and I will warrant thine intent shall be fulfilled.

This she did. The mazers realized £3 16s. 8d., but brought poor Margaret no good fortune. She then delated Lankiston to the diocesan court and he was ordered to restore the mazers or their value within eight days and to hold himself ready for further penance. For her part, Margaret was sentenced to public penance by walking in procession with bare feet and a headscarf portraying flames upon three successive Sundays.

To sum up, what late medieval English people asked of authority above all was political tranquillity and loyalty, government that would do right to all equally, family solidarity with obedience to parents, the protection of the local lord and his courts, and a happy home-life. Last, but perhaps the greatest, was the desire to protect one's reputation, to be 'of good fame'. This affected people personally and politically, and the two can scarcely be disentangled in the Middle Ages. Good fame meant respectability. To be of local political or administrative consequence meant also to be a man of some property, to be of 'livelihood', to be 'worshipful', and those who could not pass this test could not act as sureties or jurors or justices of the peace or in any other of the scores of offices which men coveted for their profit and position. But it meant more than this as well. For poor men it meant a certain protection against accusations before courts, in that others would be the more likely to swear to their innocence. It connoted stability of dwelling, in one's own household or somebody else's. For a richer man it meant greater security in political life, since politics was an intensely personal matter and proceeded all too often by personal amity on the one hand or by rumours and slander on the other: 'rumours and flying tales', as a Paston letter has it. Sir John Fastolf was suspicious of unknown gentlemen who disliked him and needed to pin down rumour-mongers by making them identify themselves, stand by what they said, and produce witnesses.* Again, politics and religious sensibility were inextricably mixed together, and the Pastons' clerical servants and friends were ever ready to apply texts of scripture to the current political situation:

> And if my good lord Warwick, with my lord his brother, Chancellor . . . would oppose . . . the writing made by them at the Coventry Parliament, they should answer for it . . . and this generally would I say at Paul's Cross if I went there. It is verified of them in Jeremiah 8. 'The lying pen of the scribes hath wrought falsehood' [*vere mendacium operatus est stilus mendax scribarum*]. . . . And I pray you think, in this Parliament, of the text of Holy Scripture, 'whosoever will not do the law of thy God and the law of the king diligently, judgement shall be executed upon him, either unto death or unto banishment, or to the confiscation of goods, or at least to prison (1 Esdras VII)'. . . .†

Underlying all was a sense that the wheel of fortune rose and fell in accordance with the will of an inscrutable Providence, as when Edward IV recovered his throne in 1471 and Sir John Paston reported the casualties and besought his servant to watch their tongues: 'The world is right queasy . . . but God hath showed Himself marvellously like Him that made all and can undo again what He likes, and I can think that by all likelihood he shall show Himself as marvellous again, and that in a short time. . . .'‡

The background to this mentality will be discussed in the last two chapters.

Paston Letters, I, No. 228; III, Nos. 723, 724.
†ibid., I, No. 355.
‡ibid., III, No. 668 (18 April 1471).

8 The Apparatus of Religion

In the twentieth century the notion of salvation has crumbled and faded under a restless and mechanized life. For every ten people who are concerned with social justice or peace on earth, possibly not more than one retains any concern with those dreadful Four Last Things which preoccupied our medieval and early modern ancestors at least occasionally during their lives: Death, Judgement, Heaven and Hell. And even those who feel they incur the risk of a future life hope for the most part, I dare say, that it will be all right on the day. So, since heaven has receded behind the cloud of scepticism, it is hard for the historical student to re-enter a world as remote as the fifteenth century and to resurrect not only the men and women of that age but the spiritual population they felt to move among them, or to vivify the eternity which seemed so close to daily life. Indeed, the fifteenth century is perhaps the most intractable age of all: not so much repellent to modern men with their tolerance, larger than that of the Victorians, as ludicrous or even contemptible in its seeming fantasies and preoccupations. In a thousand examination answers, suffused with dim memories of Huizinga or Burckhardt or Coulton, it is castigated for 'decline' or 'abuse' or 'corruption'. For over the centuries little remains in that folk memory which informs the textbook-reading public save the hectoring voice of Tetzel and the clattering of pennies in the alms-boxes as liberated souls leaped, one sardonically supposes, from the toils of Purgatory to the bliss of everlasting day.

Yet it will not do to abandon the later Middle Ages to an automatic historical scorn, allowing the age no other interest than as a dreary *point de départ* to an ever-brightening voyage into modernity. Someone should speak for it, at least to explain the landmarks of the scene. An exercise in interpretation is required, not, if the reader will allow the insistence, by way of justifying the apparatus of a reactionary religion, or of debunking the debunkers, but as a simple act of historical justice to a time that spoke a different language of the spirit.

If we speak of the later Middle Ages, or later medieval religion, as *decadent*, then we imply that what went before was in general better. The first point — and it is a historical, not a religious one — is that in referring to this 'decadent' age we are in danger of committing an error. Here our main fault as historians lies in regarding the people of every medieval century as more or less similar to each other; it lies in observing the admirable religious life of, say, the twelfth century, so well praised by writers, and imagining that by the time the fifteenth century arrived the inhabitants of Christendom, not much different from those of three hundred years before, had forgotten what was good for them, or what was pure and noble, and had sunk into inferior forms of religious practice, from which they were quite rightly rescued by reformers. If this were a sound procedure, then it would not be misleading to compare an Anselm or a Bernard with the lesser and grosser figures of immediately pre-Reformation times. Yet this kind of comparison ignores two facts: first, that the world had changed, and with it the people as a whole; and, secondly, that we are comparing the incomparable — the supreme figures of one age with the ruck of mankind in another. The argument, favoured by certain religious historians of our own day, that the late Middle Ages stand condemned simply because they did not produce great figures like Anselm or Bernard, has seemed to me an unsatisfying one and, indeed, at bottom vitiated by a curious kind of snobbery. For the splendour and the virtue of the late Middle Ages reside in this, that a vast mass of mankind in western Europe was raising itself to a higher level of education, a better individual standard of living, a more lively hope for the future, than were enjoyed by the majority of men and women in the twelfth or thirteenth centuries. In an age of first-generation literates one does not look for masters of new achievement nor condemn it for mediocrity. One waits in patience, taking pride in modest but widespread advance, expecting something more of the children then being born and put to school.

There is no doubt that St Anselm and St Bernard were greater, more perceptive, intelligent and spiritual, than the common man or even the leading men of the fifteenth century. But we forget too easily that their splendid monasteries were built and their tiny society of equals was sustained by the labours of a wretched and impoverished crowd who do not feature in the records save as a target for contumely. There is no doubt, either, that the run of fifteenth-century men were in much better case than the generality of their ancestors. Recall St Bernard, that lordly son of a lordly house, praising the magnificent austerity of monastic architecture. We may well echo his satisfaction even as we gaze round the ruins of Rievaulx or Fountains Abbey and compare them with the riot of popish ornament that became more elaborate as the Middle Ages proceeded. But Bernard readily allowed that ordinary churches must have their pictures and images and crude aids to devotion, since, as he put it, 'they cannot excite the devotion of the carnal populace with spiritual ornaments, and must employ material ones'. The aristocrat was making concessions to sensual man, for whom he hardly concealed his disdain.

Then, to fasten attention more closely upon the present subject — the late medieval period — we have to admit that it was on all hands an age of special anxiety. Every literary and artistic form tells us so. The pestilence and sudden death which actually brought social betterment to the survivors, the social mobility and conflict that resulted, the need for thousands of families to adjust themselves in one way or another to new conditions under the lowering clouds of sudden mortality, brought with them also a sense of insecurity and terror. The Scottish poet, Robert Henryson, wrote for many others when in the late fifteenth century he besought God to remove the peril of plague:

> Use derth, O Lord, or seiknes and hunger soir,
> And slaik Thy plaig that is so penetryve!
> Thy pepill are perreist: quha ma remeid thairfoir
> Bot Thow, O Lord, that for thame lost Thy lyve!*

In the visual arts, too, the Dance of Death was a *leitmotiv*. Its meaning was

*Selected Poems of Robert Henryson, edited by Charles Elliott (Clarendon Press, 1963), p. 122.

Left St Michael weighing the souls of the dead. An English alabaster group of the early fifteenth century. *Below* Pope, Emperor and King, with crowned skeletons.

not only death's inevitability. It had always been that, and the theme was not entirely new. But death appeared now to operate with a just and dreadful egalitarianism as the skeleton, scythe in hand, led the dance around and around. The scythe swept everywhere, but unpredictably and respecting none. The very improvement and fresh articulateness among great numbers of men lends this figure a more sinister meaning and encourages its more frequent employment:

> I know that the poor and the rich,
> The wise and the foolish, cleric and lay,
> Nobles and villeins, the generous and the mean,
> Big and little, handsome and homely,
> Ladies in folded-back collars,
> No matter their worldly station
> Wearing coverchiefs or cauls
> Death seizes without exception.*

Against this dark figure no saint, however local, might be left uninvoked. As for Christ Himself, his human life and suffering mirrored with a strange comfort the lot of his flock, as they painted or carved Him upon Calvary or lowered from the cross into the arms of His mother. And the mother herself seemed in consequence the most intimate and understanding protectress of mankind.

This, then, is the setting of later medieval religion, in Britain, France, the Low Countries, Germany and to a lesser extent the world south of the Alps. New men needed a new salvation, both on earth and for ever. They asked for safety in a manner more articulate and more human than before and, let us be fair to them, they had need to. But they expected to work for their salvation.

Later medieval religion was one of works as well as of faith. Little by little this preoccupation with works would seem false and wrong as dissatisfaction with its apparatus grew, and logical reflection on the infinite majesty of God suggested its absurdity. But the full day of Justification by Faith alone (*Solifidianism*) was not yet come. In the later Middle Ages men still believed they had to try for themselves. This point will be made clearer by looking at the preambles to two wills. One was written by a typical man of the fifteenth century who believed in pious works and that the saints and angels would help him if he tried to help himself and others. The second will was written at the end of the sixteenth century by a Protestant who had, of course, rejected the invocation of saints and denied the effectiveness of human striving to attain

*François Villon, *Le Testament*, lines 5—12, translated by Galway Kinnell (Signet Classics, 1965).

merit in the eyes of God, relying for his salvation upon the free and un-merited choice of God Himself. Wills are useful documents to illustrate these mental attitudes because, though they might often run in standardized form off the pens of professional clerks, many of them are *not* standardized, and they express a man's most serious feelings at, presumably, the most serious moment of his life. Here, then, is our medieval man — John Birkhede, a clerk of the Archbiship of Canterbury, who had been concerned in the founding of All Souls College, Oxford. He made his will in 1457, and began it thus:

> Since evil and short are the days of man, and the divide of death ought not to be forgotten, and death like a lurking robber rushes to seize a man, so it is that in the pain of sickness, when bitter death approaches my mind (wandering over fleeting troubles and tending to forget the salvation of my soul), I now make my will.... Composed in mind though weak in bodily strength I gaze over the past course of time from my bed, and doubt whether I am able to pay for the just judgement which none of human condition can avoid. First and especially I invoke and humbly beseech the mercy of our almighty and compassionate Saviour, Jesus Christ, that he may have mercy upon me, most wretched sinner, and may grant me time for true penitence and the bewailing of my sins; so that when I pass from this world, that ancient and pestiferous enemy of humankind shall find in me nothing wicked or hurtful (*sinistrum aut molestum*).... May there be present to my special aid, guardianship and defence the most blessed Virgin Mary, Mother of God, St John the Baptist, St Michael the Archangel, and the angel assigned to me, in order that all my thought, acts, will and senses may be disposed and subject to the will of God and of Our Lord Jesus Christ, our Saviour who condescended to suffer death for man who was lost....*

Here in a few lines is the structure of medieval religion: the immediate consciousness of death, which comes like a thief in the night; the conscious-ness of sin and the need for mercy; the fear of adverse judgement; the belief that mercy can be forthcoming through the redemption by Christ; and that the sinner may be enabled the more easily to achieve this by the help of the prayers of the Blessed Virgin and also of other saints who are already known to be pleasing to God, and of those individual, entirely spiritual yet created beings known as angels. It is a mixture of fear, faith, good works and inter-cession.

With this attitude the profoundest contrast may be seen in the will of Edward Gellibrand, minister of the English Protestant church at Middleburg, Zeeland, who retired to Oxford and died in 1598.† (It is interesting that both our testators were connected with Oxford.) Gellibrand began by commending himself, body and soul, into the hands of God, and then went on to declare:

* Somerset House, will register 'Godyn', folio 201v.
†Somerset House, will register 'Woodhall', folio 13.

... as He hath of His free grace and merit chosen me to be an heir of His kingdom and glory, and sealed me up by His Holy Spirit to the day of redemption, so He will receive my soul into His glory and raise up my body to life at the last day. ...

The effective text, it may be observed, is somewhat shorter: no mention here of sins to be expiated, for that would be an impossible task to a mere man who can do absolutely nothing which in itself is pleasing to God. Yet there is no flicker of fear either. All is left to the merit of Christ Himself who, being God and possessed of total foreknowledge, may well by His arbitrary but un-questionable choice have elected the testator to be numbered among the blessed. For all the abasement of the human condition that such words imply, there is a kind of superb confidence in them, expressed as much as anything by the indicative instead of the subjunctive mood: 'as He *hath* ... chosen ... so He *will* receive ... me'. This again is not a typically medieval voice.

But the medieval point of view needs a longer elaboration. During that epoch, and especially towards the end of it, men often thought of human life and its progress towards salvation under the image of a ladder. One climbed up, rung by rung. It required effort. It was painful, and there was always the danger of slipping down or even falling off. Conversely, one could be helped or hauled up by others, by the prayers and deliberately applied sufferings of others, whether living or dead, whether praying and sacrificing on earth, or praying in heaven. These forms of assistance were organized and authorized through the Church: Masses, Offices, pilgrimages, contributions of prayers and even money to specified good works, like the building of bridges or churches or hospitals, which earned, not pardon, but some remission of punishment due to sin already forgiven, provided the essential conditions of a good confession were fulfilled. But the image of the ladder gives the central idea. In fact, the English spiritual writer, Walter Hilton, wrote a popular book called *The Ladder of Perfection* (*Scala Perfectionis*) which set out a mode of spiritual life; and it was a book detestable to the later reformers for its title itself, which suggested a double blasphemy: first in the notion of effort, as though wicked men had any power of themselves to help themselves; and secondly, worse still, that they could dream of attaining perfection. Such was the enormous theological chasm that opened between men.

Medieval man believed in aids to salvation, and it is possible to classify these as 'personal ways', namely, the saints and angels, and the 'instrumental means', or the instruments of ecclesiastical and religious life, like the Mass, chantries and indulgences, which so deeply left their imprint upon European religious and social, economic and even political life.

However fond the late medievals were of praying to saints and placing themselves under their patronage, it remains clear that the central figure in the religious universe was that of Christ Himself, the Redeemer. In every parish church he was portrayed on the Holy Rood, the cross, flanked by the figures of St Mary his mother, and sometimes of St John the Evangelist and others. The Rood was placed between the chancel and the nave, or sometimes in the porch, and in a great number of wills testators left money to burn lights before it. Representations mostly show Christ in some suffering or sacrificial aspect of his human nature: scourged, crowned with thorns, crucified in an agonized and naturalistic posture, taken down from the cross into the arms of his weeping mother, or laid in the tomb. Nowhere more than in Germany were shameful death and physical destruction more vividly portrayed. These were the artistic preoccupations of Albrecht Dürer in his terrible woodcuts, and it is all of a piece that Dürer depicted human death in the same terms, as in his famous 'Ritter, Tod und Teufel'. Allied with this concentration on the passion of Christ were the devotions to the Precious Blood, relics of which were enshrined at Bruges and elsewhere, and to the Way of the Cross which provided a popular meditation for layfolk.

After Christ came the figure of the Blessed Virgin. The late Middle Ages saw a tremendous expansion of Marian devotion in western Europe, particularly lavished upon a protectress who flung about her suppliants a mantle against death and disaster. The images in parish churches also reflect this. Testators willed that lights should burn before the image of Our Lady, especially under the title of Our Lady of Pity, Our Lady Help of Christians, Our Lady of Perpetual Succour. Such an image, encrusted with jewels and surrounded with burning candles, stood in the chapel of St Mary of the Pew in St Stephen's Chapel, Westminster (where the Commons met), and before which kings of England prayed privately; for in this image they were said to place great trust, whether it was Richard II on the fateful day in 1381 when he met the rebels at Smithfield, or Prince Henry, who made his confession to the anchorite there on the evening of his father's death in 1413. This is a single example, chosen because it exemplifies the devotion and example of the king himself. But everywhere devotion to the Blessed Virgin took pride of place among the saints. In the earliest surviving will register kept by the commissary-general of Canterbury, dating from the fifteenth century, there are 146 testaments in which specific bequests are made to maintain lights before particular saints or their altars. Of these, thirty-four specially singled out lights before the Rood and forty lights before the image of the Virgin. Other similar bequests were relatively much fewer: sixteen before one or other of the St Johns, ten before St Catherine, and fewer still before other saints.

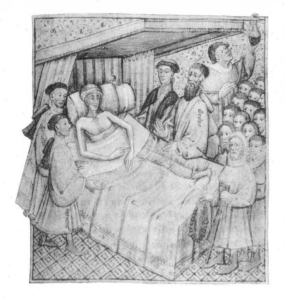

Above left The deathbed of Richard Whittington, 1430. *Above right* Our Lady of Pity. *Below left* The deposition from the Cross. *Below right* Death Riding. Drawing by Dürer, 1505.

During the fifteenth century, councils and theologians were arguing about the subtle doctrine of the Immaculate Conception. The Dominicans were against it, and a group of them at Berne got into serious trouble for a rather ridiculous demonstration against it, when they disguised themselves as heavenly apparitions who announced that Our Lady was conceived in sin. Four of these were discovered by the Inquisition and burned as heretics in 1509. But though the doctrine was not promulgated until the nineteenth century, it may properly be said that common consensus favoured it and that the popularity of Mary was much less imposed on the Church from above than hoisted up from below by a wealth of ordinary devotion that saw in her a supreme parallel with the 'good lordship' men sought on earth, where a powerful intercessor might so often put in a good word, achieve a benefit or avoid calamity. More extremely, the figure of Mary, half-mother, half-intercessor, might seem in an age of rare suicide an alternative to despair itself. It was small wonder that collections of her miracles circulated freely, like *Les Miracles de Notre Dame* by Jean Miélot, secretary to the Duke of Burgundy, or that her image was worn, in the early days of printing in Germany, as a sort of talisman against the plague — *Pestblätter*, as they were called.

After Mary came a whole host of saints and angels, each with his or her local popularity. They are too numerous to list or analyse here, though one should recall that their historical credentials were sometimes very shaky, and the group of Jesuit scholars called the Bollandists have had fun with them, as in the case of the Eleven Thousand Virgins of whom the late Father Grosjean remarked, 'You see, there was a mistake, both as to quantity and quality.' But perhaps a historical point may be made by referring to the cultus of St Anne, mother of Mary, favoured by the Carmelites and for whom Erasmus in his youth was, as he tells us, 'devoured by piety'. For this proliferation of the Holy Family, extravagant though it seems, reflects the intensely strong family feeling of the age and provided a mirror and exemplar of what people felt to be fundamental in their own lives. It is curious to think that the function sometimes said to be fulfilled in modern times by the royal family was not in the Middle Ages performed by the king's household but by that of Nazareth, and some may regard this, clouded in the mists of antiquity and invention, as the safer model.

Just as the Redeemer was the personal centre of fifteenth-century religion, despite the sometimes morbid one-sidedness of his portrayal, so the primary means of approaching him in formal worship was through the sacrifice of the Mass. The Mass, also a memorial of the Last Supper with its implications of social brotherhood, had this aspect of it quite overshadowed during our period and long afterwards by its sacrificial quality. It was the sacrifice of God-made-man on Calvary, not repeated but renewed and continued in time. Undoubtedly there were abuses. There was on many sides an unduly mechanical notion of the physical benefits and effects of the Mass, the superstitious belief that to attend Mass would be rewarded with material favours. There was also a superstition of arithmetic, that special benefits lay in the celebration of certain favoured numbers of Masses — three, or seven, or the Gregorian Trental, which is to say, thirty Masses. A strange story concerns a bishop who suffered from gout and was presented with a block of ice which some fishermen had dragged from the sea thinking it to be a fish. (The fish, of course, was an ancient symbol of Christ, from the Greek letters for *icthus* meaning 'fish' and standing for 'Jesus Christ, Son of God, Saviour'.) About to rest his foot upon it, the bishop was alarmed to hear a shrill voice within which informed him that a departed soul was being punished for its sins by incarceration in the ice. The bishop thereupon celebrated a trental of Masses and so obtained the release of the soul to heaven. Irrelevant ideas like this were sometimes incorporated into books of piety. Nicholas of Cusa had to probibit such books in his diocese of Brixen in 1455, and Jean Gerson, Chancellor of the University of Paris, was loud in his scorn for the idea of assured temporal advantages. Yet other devotional writings of a more balanced sort emphasized the proper value of hearing Mass with right intentions:

> What man be clean out of sin
> And hear a Mass when it begin,

to him would accrue the 'meeds' or rewards of the Mass. There was, as ever, a historical division between popular and official theology; though again, to be fair to the fifteenth century in general, the simple-minded could often distinguish better than is sometimes supposed. One of the most popular vernacular books of devotion in German-speaking lands, the *Seelenführer*, or *Guide of the Soul*, of 1498, announced, 'There is no need to believe all the wonders we read of in the pious books.'

One principal fact is undeniable, that the later Middle Ages saw a great multiplication of private Masses, offered by large numbers of priests at private altars, without congregations, for the welfare of the living and the dead, and especially for the families and benefactors of those who were supporting the priest. This institution of the private Mass, is, of course, connected with the doctrine of Purgatory, and it meant the growth of the chantry system, perhaps the most typical religious institution of the late Middle Ages.

The doctrine of Purgatory was not new. It was taught in a fairly well-

Mass for the dead; an early fifteenth-century view.

formed and coherent way even in patristic times that men who died in a state of grace — that is, of regret for their sins — still had to pay in some kind of temporary suffering the price of the sins they had committed. Or, to put it another way, that the temporary sufferings of this intermediate state called Purgatory were necessary and even desired by the soul in order to make it possible to bear the intensity of the beatific vision in heaven. Purgatory was no joke, and books of devotion, not to say Dante's *Purgatorio*, conjure up visions of pains so fearful that hell itself seemed hardly worse, save for the absence in hell of faith, charity and hope. (But there, perhaps, is all the difference possible.) However this may be, a further idea was that the sufferings of Purgatory could be mitigated, or abbreviated, by the prayers and good works of others, whether loving well-wishers still on earth, or intercessors already in heaven. Since people took this scheme of things very seriously, and since family solidarity was one of the fundamental social facts of the age, what better work, what piety more excellent, than to arrange for Mass to be said for the benefit of the souls in Purgatory, and especially the souls of father, mother, kinsmen, ancestors and benefactors? The theological point lay in the supreme value of the Mass, for that was an application of Christ's own suffering and sacrifice which were infinite and no mere human work, since Christ was God.

It was upon this twin stream of development that the chantry system was built: the high view of the sacrifice of the Mass, together with family solidarity. It ought to be added that chantries were things which the average prosperous individual of the fifteenth century could afford. No longer was it the age *par excellence* of the monasteries, which only the very rich could endow, nor of the friars, though these were still popular. The chantry was something private and personal in an age of a developing middle class. It might mean a splendid college of priests, or an elaborate and beautiful chapel like that of Bishop Alcock in Ely Cathedral. But these were the exceptions numerically. Mostly, chantries were altars, or a share in the use of an altar, in some parish church or chapel. Such a chantry would involve the regular service of a single chaplain who might get £10 or £11 a year. In a big and important college of priests, which existed for the same theological purpose, the chaplains, or canons, would get more. Again, St Stephen's chapel at Westminster provides a good example. It had been re-founded by Edward III in 1348 as his palace chapel, with a dean and twelve canons. The progress of its building followed the fortunes of the royal finances, proceeding sometimes quickly but at times of stringency held up, with the unfinished parts covered with straw to protect them from decay. When finished, the building contained a lower chapel for the public and an upper one in which the king liked to

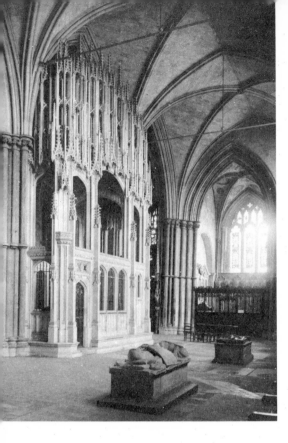

Tomb and chantry chapel of Bishop Waynflete (d. 1486) in Winchester Cathedral.

worship, entering it from his palace. Here in the upper part was the famous closet called St Mary of the Pew, containing the image of the Virgin, encrusted with jewels which no jeweller could appraise. It was in the care of a clerk, one of whose duties was to teach children near by, and one day a child was told to put out the candles for the day but accidentally caused a fire in doing so, and the ornaments were burnt. The chapel was rebuilt in the 1460s by Lord Rivers, kinsman of Edward IV, who obtained large indulgences for the chapel from the Pope, equivalent to those that could be acquired at the ancient private chapel of the Popes at the head of the *Scala Santa* in Rome. The Dean and Canons of St Stephens were privileged, well-beneficed and well-to-do clerks, servants of the king and of great men. The last dean was the king's physician, Dr John Chambers. Dean and Canons were allowed to be absent during a large part of the year, but still received substantial salaries. When they made their wills they, as well as others, often left bequests to the chapel which often invested the money in house property in the City and elsewhere, remembering the benefactors in the year's liturgical observances.* St Stephen's Chapel, then, was at the social apex of the chantry system, but there were innumerable others of less account, all more or less well endowed and with funds invested in real property for the support of chaplains. In the fifteenth century such chantries came to be regarded as legal corporations, and collectively they were very rich. They acted in this way as a drain upon the capital accumulation of propertied people who often left to them a considerable proportion of their savings. This ought to be borne in mind when we reflect upon the fury with which reformers attacked Masses for the dead, for behind the loud cries against superstition – genuinely enough meant – it is hard not to discern also the outrage of substantial men who felt that funds had been misappropriated and could with advantage be taken back again.

In the same category as chantries came indulgences, which were granted by ecclesiastical authorities for the performance of prescribed works of piety. Popes began to exploit this source of revenue much more thoroughly at the time of the Great Schism (1378–1417), and although they were careful to safeguard the essential spiritual conditions of good confession and right intention, the system was open to wide abuse. To take one instance, the Cistercian abbots of Fountains and Leicester wrote in 1500 to the Abbot of Citeaux complaining that some of the younger members of the Order had applied for leave to go to the Roman court for their Jubilee Indulgence because they were actuated by curiosity and levity rather than devotion, and rarely did English monks or laymen derive either health or devotion from a visit to Rome. Another impression is that at the very end of the Middle Ages indulgences were more often being granted in return for works of secular and social value, like repairing damage done to Norham Castle by the Scots in 1514. In any case, indulgences were becoming less popular with English people after the middle of the fifteenth century. Like Langland before him, Erasmus had his doubts when he wrote, 'I don't speak slightingly of indulgences themselves, but I laugh at the folly of my fuddling companion who chose rather to venture the whole stress of his salvation upon a skin of parchment than upon the amendment of his life.'

Enough has now been said to characterize the external quality of later medieval religion. This may be summed up by referring to the new public, its sense of insecurity, its belief in human striving, its middle-class family solidarity. Much may rightly be made of the little devotions like pilgrimages

---

*The endowment of obits is recorded in a register of the fifteenth century, now British Museum Cottonian MS. Faustina B VIII, folios 8–53.

and rosaries as well as the more central institutions of chantry Masses and indulgences, and the unduly mechanical spirit which all this apparatus so easily engendered in the general public, though it is also fair to be sceptical about the general public's spirituality at any time in history.

Yet there is still a point to be made about the development of religion which has nothing to do with external devotions, and nothing directly to do with criticisms of it by heretics, rebels and reformers. This may be called the 'growth of religious intention' or, to put it differently, the growth of conscience. For there can be discerned in the fourteenth and fifteenth centuries a genuine elevation of human standards behind all the superstition, mediocrity and abuse. This does not notably apply to bishops and princes of the church, though there were some good ones, for there had been better in earlier centuries, as was pointed out at the beginning of this chapter. Nor does it especially apply to cloistered religious, though again there were some good ones, like Carthusians. It applies rather to the submerged yet faintly articulate

An English pilgrim, c. 1360. Wall-painting from Forthampton Court, near Tewkesbury.

157

public for whom Piers the Plowman was a spokesman, and also to many parish priests and the people who heard them preach sermons and who prepared themselves for confession with the aid of new booklets in the vernacular tongue. Piers the Plowman can scarcely have been speaking in a void, in spite of the fact, or because of the fact, that he was a religious and poetic genius. He was not only the social satirist who amplified a more ancient sense of social wrong. He expressed religious ideas which others of his day were thinking and feeling. To his readers the vision of salvation and damnation made sense, or they would not have read him. For them the two roads were revealed by Holy Church. These were not the ways of rosaries and indulgences, but of Dowel and Do-bet. The road to damnation was to follow Lady Meed, loving worldly reward above all else. The other way was through repentance and in response to conscience and good deeds; and who does these, he wrote, shall go to eternal life. Many of his readers would recognize the words of the Athanasian Creed which he used, for it was familiar to that growing company which followed the Offices in the Roman or Sarum rite:

> Et qui bona egerunt, ibunt in vitam eternam,
> Qui vero mala, in ignem eternum.*

In one famous and obscure scene, Piers tears up the Pope's pardon, and this has been convincingly interpreted to mean that the mere parchment, the mere form of words, was nothing. He will accept the Pope's pardon in itself, but asserts that it is useless if divorced from moral action. Repentance and amendment first, and then might come the pardon. Faith without works is dead. And works for Piers meant more than money tinkling into the box, for salvation cannot be bought without some glimmer of right intention, however important the objects for which the money was intended:

> As to trust to these triennals, trewly methinketh
> Is nought so siker for the soul . certis as is Dowel. . . .

This is what Erasmus was to say.

Elsewhere, too, in the *Vision of Piers the Plowman*, a role is assigned to Conscience, which is the activating will of a man, informed by Reason. In the A Text, the first version, Conscience is a layman and a warrior; in the B Text it is not Conscience but Reason who preaches repentance; in the C Text is written

> In my conscience I know . what Christ wills me to do.

*'And they that have done good, shall go into life everlasting; and they that have done evil, into everlasting fire.'

Finally, there is the sermon literature of the age. Only a minority may have read Langland's great poem, but thousands of people went to sermons, and we know from the manuscripts that have been collected and studied by Dr G. R. Owst what the contents of these sermons were likely to be. The fifteenth century was not so great an age of sermon *exempla* as the fourteenth, and a lot of earlier ones must have been in use even then. But there is one particular collection from the fifteenth century which is useful in gauging the mentality of the time. This is a little book by Alexander Carpenter called *The Destruction of Vices (Destructio Vitiorum)*. It was put together in final form somewhere about 1429, and its popularity is proved by the fact that it was printed in Cologne, Nuremberg and Paris several times by the early sixteenth century. Carpenter was critical of many things in the Church, but he was no Lollard. Above all, he believed in preaching as 'the greatest and most excellent work of mercy'. Greater than the 'earthquake' of physical science or the 'fire' of human knowledge was 'the gentle breeze of Holy Scripture', for it contained the teaching of divine law, which so many pastors rejected for more lucrative and plausible knowledge. To his lay congregations Carpenter said they should know the Gospel, for this was worth all the mechanisms of piety: 'And even if some men who kneel before images and demand deliverance and help from them are sometimes healed, yet, if they believe that this is due to the virtue and potency of the image, they are certainly deceived. . . .'

They were serious men, these preachers, and the note deepens as they speak of the life and death of man. One can hardly doubt that in this last long simile there is a sharp and healthy blending of attitudes: of scepticism towards the mere externals of a religion grown dangerously elaborate, and a wholly orthodox belief in the supremacy of conscience, which is to be examined before it is too late:

As in the case of a clock, the clock-maker places one pin in a certain wheel, and when it reaches a certain point in the clock, immediately the mechanism is released; and then all the bells strike, and the figures in the semblance of clerks and priests pass by in procession chanting. But how long do these things last? Assuredly, until the weight reaches the ground, and no longer. For, after the weight has been grounded, everything immediately stops. So, spiritually, God who is the guardian of man puts a pin in him, that is to say, he ordains a limit to his life which he cannot pass. And, therefore, when man reaches that limit, immediately he is dissolved by death; and then the bells toll and priests and clerks chant his exequies. But for how long does this din last, think you? Truly, until the weight, that is to say, his ponderous body, has reached the ground. And then when his corpse is cast into the earth, immediately the tumult ceases, and the dead man passes into oblivion.

9 The Flight from Intellect

In 1463 François Villon, reprieved from the death penalty, disappeared finally into the squalor of Paris. What, one may ask, has he to do with the mind and spirit of the late medieval Church — the subject of this last chapter — save that he was a clerk and a graduate, and also, let us confess, a 'social failure' and a condemned criminal? The answer is that he was an immortal poet who in writing for his own day wrote in some measure for ours, which also sees the assured forces of reason and established order in some disarray and dissolving in a kind of social turbulence and philosophical scepticism:

> Twisted men dispossessed of reason,
> Unnatural and fallen from knowledge,
> Empty of sense and full of unreason,
> Deluded fools stuffed with emptiness. . . .

Yet at the same time he wrote of a teeming urban life where men and women of many nations and classes mingled, of high fashion among irreverent youth, of the shadow of death, and of love. The pimp and the thief wrote poetry which displays a morality of the highest nature, which is that of tolerance, and his tolerance rested upon the highest of human virtues, which is the admission of ignorance about other people. He would have agreed with Sir Thomas Browne: 'No man can justly censure or condemn another, because indeed no man truly knows another.' He wrote therefore of pardon.

> To Carthusians and Celestines
> To Mendicants and Devotes,
> To star-gazers and clock-watchers,
> To serving girls and pretty sluts
> In jackets and tight-fitting coats,
> To cocky fellows drooping with love,
> Happily fitted with tawny boots,
> I cry to all men pardon.

In the previous chapter I gave reasons and illustrations for regarding this

Left François Villon, from a woodcut published in 1489. *Right* Warden and scholars of New College, Oxford. Founded in 1379 to make good 'the fewness of the clergy, arising from pestilences, wars and other miseries of the world', the college is here shown *c.* 1460.

epoch as an age of anxiety and the endeavours to overcome it in a world where temporal and eternal ambitions were strangely intermixed. In this last chapter I want to take up this explanation on a different level. The title of the chapter needs some justification. It is not that reason, skill and innovation were lacking, but the fifteenth century was scarcely an 'Age of Intellect'. Here again, the statement has no pejorative intent. Intellect in the sense intended has a certain confident assurance which is not unmixed with spiritual pride. Although we have begun with poetry, that was merely the sugar on the philosophical pill that is to come. For the primary purpose of this final section is to show, at least in outline, how the spiritual and theological assurance of the earlier Middle Ages had broken down.

Perhaps such an excursion into intellectual history by one who is no professional philosopher is a very dubious and marginal proceeding; perhaps, in any case, the philosophical ideas of a handful of university men in the fourteenth and fifteenth centuries can hardly have been of much consequence in Christendom at large – can hardly have affected the man and woman in the parish church or the inn, or the temper of the whole age. But this would be a wrong suspicion. There is undoubtedly *some* relationship between the thoughts and writings of intellectuals and the common assumptions of common men. Philosophers themselves are, after all, men in the street with a more trained power of rationalizing what a lot of people obscurely or instinctively feel to be true or untrue. Like poets and novelists, they speak for their time, and this is why, as historians, we must occasionally study them.

So it was in the fourteenth and fifteenth centuries, when European men began to be much less certain about the powers of the human intellect to know about God and his existence, about the logical architecture of the universe, about the role of human reason in providing a solid ground for revealed religion and even for moral behaviour.

To put briefly, in the proverbial nutshell and at the beginning, the whole burden of what I am about to say, I suggest that in the later Middle Ages people became much more sceptical about the capacity of the human intellect to reach certainty in all those matters we term *abstractions*, or which medieval philosophers called universals: such matters as justice, right and wrong, God himself and, of course, the doctrines taught by the Church.

This does not imply that the age was full of sceptics and agnostics in the modern sense. Occasionally a monastic chronicler would gloomily attribute some natural disaster to men's unbelief in God.* But these were words, not

---

* *Historia Anglicana*, ii, p. 12.

metaphysical explanations. There were probably very few professional agnostics, and philosophers and theologians who found themselves doubting the basis in natural reason for the doctrines of religion went to some lengths in asserting their own faith. This was rarely, if ever, hypocrisy or cowardice. It was simply that they went on believing, or acting as though they believed, which is sometimes the same thing, and also because religion was still so intimately part of the social and political and emotional framework of life that self-conscious rejection was scarcely thinkable. We might also observe that the most radical and corrosive thinkers were themselves priests and religious, and that the ideas which have been revived in our own midst by professional atheists in the universities of London or Oxford were excogitated 600 years ago within the heart of Europe's theological faculties.

These critical ideas obviously affected the general quality of late medieval religion. It was on the whole a less *rational* religion than it had been among the great schoolmen of thirteenth-century Paris and Oxford and their educated followers. The effect on the mass of mankind may be estimated by what has been said in the previous chapter. For most people, as always, religion was held and lived on a relatively low intellectual plane, however intense the spiritual life of the saints and mystics. Later medieval religion was exceedingly practical: a religion of good works and simple faith. For a few, more elevated spirits, it was mystical, and meant a life of prayer and self-denial rewarded by a burning and intuitive knowledge and direct love of God. For these, mysticism may perhaps be defined in the words of a modern novelist: 'unmediated communion with whomever controls you'.* But even the brilliant intellectuals and the saintly men, like Nicholas of Cusa, felt (with a few exceptions) less confident than their thirteenth-century forbears, and overwhelmed by the majestic unknowableness of the Creator and his works. And this sense of God's inaccessibility is perhaps the hall-mark of the age, leading in one direction to a *philosophical* scepticism and in another to an impatience with the ancient apparatus of priestly and sacramental mediation. It is worth remembering this, not only for its own sake, as a way of understanding the last years of the Middle Ages, but in order to help us understand the reformers and protestants who were to come; for they were the heirs of the later schoolmen, and their efforts were efforts to find again that which had been lost.

In order to explain this in greater detail, we must return for a while to the

* Words used, if my recollection is correct, by Mr John Le Carré in a BBC television interview, February 1966.

problem of universals. One of the things which appear to distinguish men from animals is man's power of language. Even if we agree that animals communicate, then they do so only in a very simple way, for example by demonstrating elementary feelings of fear or grief, pleasure or rage in the face of situations that are either 'nice' or 'nasty'. Their communications would be limited to the demonstrative. They make signs that signify 'danger', or 'alas', or 'lovely'. Men, however, frame propositions. They do this by using words, which signify generalized experiences, or concepts. If I say to you, 'The unpleasant man came into the room,' I am, of course, describing an act of great simplicity (combined with a value-judgement); yet the description is not a simple act by a dog's standard, because it involves the utterance of a series of terms which presuppose some generalized experience communicable between individuals: *unpleasant, man, room, came into*. Even a noun referring to something particular and concrete like 'room' is in a sense an abstraction, and all these intelligible generalities put together are needed to communicate an idea which in itself is quite simple and individual.

Words, therefore, in distinction from inarticulate cries, have a special kind of meaning, passionless and universal. The word 'man' has some kind of meaning, or status, or reality. But what kind of reality? This is the age-old problem of Universals, or, as we may more understandably call it, of Abstractions, which so exercised medieval thinkers, and has never in one way or another ceased to interest philosophers. In medieval form, the usual question to be asked was, 'Are the things which abstractions signify in any sense real?' Is there such a thing as mankind? We know there are objects walking about which we call men, but when we refer to mankind do we refer to anything that has a real existence? Those medieval thinkers who held universal terms to represent realities were, in scholastic language, called Realists. Those, on the other hand, who said that universal terms were only names, noises, mental constructions put into sound to serve as a kind of mental shorthand for the purposes of communication, were called Nominalists.

The question, 'Are Universals real?' may even seem today rather a silly one. Most moderns are instinctively Nominalists, and I doubt whether there are any thoroughgoing Realists any more. But perhaps the fair-minded historian will agree that the question is not so silly as at first sight it may seem if two things are pointed out, the one a practical point, and the other a historical one. First, the practical matter: it is easy enough to agree that only men are 'real' whilst mankind is simply a name without the same kind of 'reality', that is to say, without any *being* of its own, without any *metaphysical* status as opposed to a purely logical status. But what about a concept like Responsibility? Or Morality? Or Justice? Are there such things as these? If we deny it, if we say 'There is no such thing as Justice, but there are only acts which, by a kind of habitual consent, everybody agrees to possess a quality of niceness called justice,' then we may appear to have adopted a kind of moral relativism. If there is no real (though abstract) standard or canon of justice, how then can we rationally and logically blame other people who act according to evidently different standards, ones which even by our standards are flagrantly unjust ones, yet still claim that they are applying justice? For such people may genuinely believe that some acts are just which we think to be unjust, whether it is, for example, the extermination of the Jews, or the killing of physically imperfect children, or anything else. It is, of course, a metaphysical point I am writing about, not a moral one. The same kind of problem would be presented by other universal terms which refer to qualities and relationships rather than simple collectivities like mankind: by terms like Goodness, or even Space and Time. Is Space 'real'? It certainly cannot be individuated, like men out of mankind, nor does it stand for a collectivity of individual things. It cannot be smelt or seen or heard or touched. This leads into deep waters, and we shall wade out no further, but it may be agreed that some problems exist here which were at least worth thinking about for medieval philosophers.

We pass to the historical point. This concerns Greek thought in general, and Plato in particular, upon whose thought so many medieval and modern ideas were based. For Plato held that all the particular and individual things of which we are aware in the world about us were copies, more or less imperfect, of perfect and indestructible ideas, or Forms, laid up, so to say, in heaven. It was by this means that he sought to explain the similarities we discern amongst things, and the greater or less conformity they show to the perfect or ideal exemplar. According to this explanation, an act would be more or less just in that it conformed, or failed to conform, with eternal Justice. The Greeks had an immense respect for intellect, for the power of abstraction, and they thought that the more abstract and intellectual the object of our thoughts, the *more* not *less* 'real' it was. For these abstractions are not subject to corruption and decay, nor to the limitations, finiteness and imperfection of individual things. The world of ideas is the pattern upon which the other universe — that of sense-perception — is made. It is the universe of being, of goodness, wisdom, truth, intellect, justice, eternity and peace, which are primordial, and of which it is only the effects which are manifest in time and place.

This attitude, this reverential posture before ideas as such, was eagerly adopted by Christian thinkers in the early Middle Ages. And although he was not a Platonist so much as an Aristotelian, there was in Thomas Aquinas, the most systematic of all medieval writers on theology, enough of this conviction of the power of the human intellect to apprehend objective, eternal truths for him to be convincingly called an Intellectualist.

We must dwell for a short while on Aquinas's attitude to intellect, because he provides a suitable norm of early and central medieval thought against which the later medieval changes can best be measured. Aquinas insisted on the absolute value of the act of intelligence. This is one of his master-ideas. If we wish to sum it up in a formula, it could be this: 'Intelligence is, for Aquinas, the faculty of the real.' (He would add, theologian as he primarily was, that it was the faculty of the real because it was the faculty of the divine, but we may leave this aside in the present context.) His system, a scholastic one which argued authority against authority and decided the issue according to a reasoned assessment of their comparative weights, was to rationalize the divine. It is scarcely surprising, then, that for Aquinas the most essential attribute of God was not his goodness, nor his will, but Being itself. God is. In the beginning was the Word — not the Deed, nor the Will. God is intelligence and reason. Furthermore, his creation, the Universe, conforms with his reasonable being, and it is arranged in necessary conformity with laws which are not merely chance patterns or occurrences that God has imposed or allowed to come into existence, but could not be otherwise because the Creator is himself reasonable. Reason, of course, is a word used by men. But man is made in the image of God and is endowed with some power of reason, which is that which makes him truly a man; and hence, man's reason is capable, however imperfectly or intermittently or fogged by passion or bad habits, of grasping objective and eternal truths — the reasonable architecture of existence. As Aquinas would say, his intelligence can *acquire* reality. Man in a sense *becomes* what he knows, as his intellect seizes, grasps and penetrates it. He is able

> To seize, to clutch, to penetrate,
> Expert beyond experience.

Yet man cannot do this immediately and intuitively as, according to the thought of the time, the angels could. Angels, to employ a metaphor, were the eagles that could stare at the sun, whilst men were the owls blinking painfully in the light. Men have to operate through *concepts*. The concept is the natural human substitute for the pure intellectual process, the pure intellectual vision we shall one day enjoy, and which the angels enjoy in heightened

St Thomas Aquinas (d. 1274). 'So far as man by creation shares in intelligence, he is made in the specific image of God.'

measure. Through concepts we apprehend particular sciences and systems. The final end of man, the vision of God, is for Aquinas essentially an intellectual one of pure speculation; for even love must perceive what it loves before it can love. According to this way of thinking, the human intellect is philosophically superior to the human will, because the intellect by grasping and understanding can possess Being itself; whereas by willing something we are at a further remove, only *desiring* to have a relationship with a Being which remains beyond us. Once the being is possessed and known, the will is accomplished.

It might be added, though it is a digression from the main argument, that Aquinas gave a higher place to the activity of the will in the ordinary moral, human order on earth. Although the true end of man is vision, or speculation, he would say that because human nature is corrupted by original sin, and men are imperfect and their vision clouded and distorted through evil, they must be rescued and put on the right path by obedience to moral imperatives.

Moving further, Aquinas held that God's existence was demonstrable by the process of human reason, and not something we could only know through special, direct revelation. It is available to all men to know that God is, and he spends some time in the first part of his *Summa Theologica* in showing how this is so, through the famous Five Ways, or arguments, for a being that is necessary, a starting-point of causality, and so on. These, of course, are not regarded as 'proofs' in the modern scientific sense, because they cannot coerce the assent of the thinker, and they have, unlike a simple mathematical proposition, to establish something which is not tautological, that is to say, they have to establish a supposed truth which is above and beyond the data supplied in the first place. But the Thomist demonstrations were held, and are held by many, to show that the existence of God is not only not contrary to reason, but is the only explanation available to human reason for existence itself.

This intellectualist philosophy of which I have been writing was enjoying its heyday in the thirteenth century, in the universities of Paris and Oxford and in the Dominican convents of Christendom. It came to be known as the 'Old Way' — the *Via Antiqua* — when times changed. This label was intended to point the contrast with the new mode of thought that became powerful from the early fourteenth century onwards — the *Via Moderna*, associated above all with the name of William of Ockham.

Ockham's ideas were not all brand new. Such is not the nature of philosophy, whose problems continuously recur. There had been men who had been thinking along similar lines long before, such as the famous Roscelin of Compiègne in the early twelfth century, who opposed the Realists and held that only sense experience could be our warrant for reality. But in Ockham we have an immensely powerful and critical mind, which not

William of Ockham (d. 1349) shown in a contemporary sketch. 'I say, therefore, that intuitive knowledge is proper individual knowledge . . .'

only founded a school of thought but may be said to have changed the direction of European attitudes.

Ockham was born about 1300, and probably at the little Surrey village of that name. The external facts of his life are soon told. He became a Franciscan friar, by then perhaps the most learned group of men in the world, and he went to study at Oxford. Although he went through all the stages and exercises for his master's degree, he never formally took it up and is sometimes therefore known as the 'Venerable Inceptor'. ('Inceptor' was the title of a man about to take his Mastership.) He wrote a great mass of works, especially on logical and political problems. In 1324 he was summoned to the papal court at Avignon to answer certain accusations of heretical teaching, and he was there for some time, for such matters moved slowly when it was a question of aberrant academic ideas rather than socially destructive activities. But a few years later he fled from Avignon and joined the court of the German Emperor Ludwig (Louis of Bavaria), who was then engaged in the last of the medieval political struggles between pope and emperor; and so Ockham joined a curious and brilliant band of men who had in various ways fallen foul of the Avignon papacy and the established order, and who had collected round the principal political opposition of the day. Ockham's later years are obscure. After the emperor's death, Ockham prepared a form of submission to the Church, but it is not known if he ever signed it. He seems to have had a typical academic reluctance to commit himself. He died at Munich in 1349, apparently of the Black Death.

Ockham took an entirely different view of the problem of universals, and one to which modern philosophers have in general been much more sympathetic than to those of the earlier Realists or Thomists. For Ockham, universals or abstractions, like 'mankind' and 'justice' and so on, were only terms. His philosophy, often called 'extreme Nominalism', is also and perhaps better called 'Terminism'. The term, he held, signified only an individual thing, and stood for it in a proposition. Only individual things exist. The very fact that something exists means that it must be an individual: a man, a dog, a particular object. There cannot be existent universals. To say that universals exist outside the mind is folly.

One ought to say in fairness to Aquinas, lest occasion for gross misunderstanding has been given in this highly simplified narrative, that he himself did not hold that there were real concrete universals floating round the heavens in a crude, physical way. How then did Aquinas and Ockham differ? They differed because Aquinas, observing similarities between particular things, gave a metaphysical explanation of these similarities. He

169

held that God creates things belonging to the same *species*, like men or apes or trees, with similar natures, in accordance with the divine Idea of human nature or ape nature or tree nature. God does not act arbitrarily. He is the supreme and intelligent spirit, and he has the knowledge, or the idea of man, and so this idea of man, of human nature, has a reality in the divine mind which is in a sense prior to the existence of individual men. The divine idea is a sort of necessary intermediate stage of existence between God the creator and the individual creatures. In this way *species*, although abstract or universal, possess reality. If this were not so, then God would have to be thought of as creating each individual man, ape, tree and so on as totally new ideas or acts, and his creativity could not be said to be in accordance with any kind of law, but only with a great number of arbitrary and unrelated acts.

But Ockham would have none of this. For him there was no need for this intermediate stage. Nothing should be supposed to exist unless there were evidence to the senses for its existence. The famous phrase attributed to Ockham (though it seems to have been coined by one of his followers) ran: 'beings ought not to be multiplied unnecessarily': *entia non multiplicanda praeter necessitatem*. This is 'Ockham's Razor', with which the new, sceptical logicians cut all speculative abstractions like 'species' out of the scheme of reality. Why, they asked, should we allow reality to these abstractions for which there is no evidence? To Ockham, the only explanation for the similarities we observe among particular individuals, like men, must be the divine choice. He believed in God, but could see no reason why God should have arranged matters as he did other than because he simply willed it so.

This leads us on to Ockham's glorification of the will of God at the expense of his reasonableness. He did not care for the idea that God should be subject to any system of law. It should be added that Ockham was more interested in logic than metaphysics: that is, he was interested in the processes of the human mind rather than the nature of ultimate reality. And indeed, he felt himself compelled to deny the capacity of men's minds to grasp beyond the concrete experience of the senses to non-material being. Logic deals with terms and names. The human mind can only know individual things, and verbal expressions are no more than conventional signs. The mistake the older philosophers had made was to confuse names with things. Hence, Justice and Responsibility and suchlike concepts are only words signifying relations between things, and not things themselves. They are nouns that enter the structure of mental propositions. You do not, he would say, add anything to your knowledge if you look at a white cloth and suppose that it is only a tiny and imperfect example of some ideal and superlative whiteness. On the contrary, if you use a general term like 'whiteness' you are speaking of something that can only be *confusedly* known, whereas if you employ a particular term, like 'this white cloth', then you are speaking of something that can be *distinctly* known.

If we consider this line of thought, it will be plain that Ockham was creating a very large gap between philosophy and theology. Philosophers of his school, who did not wish to deny the Christian religion, had at the same time no rational means by which they could jump from the particularity all about them to a sure knowledge of the eternal and spiritual. Faith remained, but the rational props were weakened or kicked away. And this too had its consequences in men's interpretation of the moral law. Confronted with a world which was obviously subject to evil and limitation, and believing in a God who by definition was infinitely powerful, the explanation could only be that God was subject to no law but acted wholly at his own good pleasure. Will, not law, must be his essential attribute. Even those things which we agree in seeing as right and just could, did God but choose to arrange it so, be wrong and unjust. Our conformity with the moral law is therefore an exercise in obedience, not in rationality. Moral behaviour turns out to be legalism, not conformity with a fundamental rightness of things duly understood by an intelligent conscience. God himself could not be reduced to any glorified likeness of human rationality.

This situation was put succinctly, though in a rather unfriendly fashion, in the fine opening chapter by the Abbé Henri Bremond in his *Histoire littéraire du sentiment religieux en France*:

The Ockhamists were not rebels but cared ardently to uphold in the face of ever-threatening naturalism, in the face of eternal paganism, the fundamental teaching of Christianity: the gratuitousness, the transcendence ... of the divine gift which makes us children of God. From these essential truths they drew unacceptable consequences, regarding in the harshest way the rights of God, the principles of morals, the misery of fallen man: a terrible God, fashioning at his mere will moral laws which he could just as well replace with a quite contradictory code; human intelligence reasoning in the void, condemned to produce only abstract concepts, merely words [*nomina*], incapable of attaining any reality. Faith was in flagrant contradiction with reason, supernature with nature. To be brief: in religion, terror; in morals, rigorism; in philosophy, scepticism. Doubtless Luther and Calvin enhanced this anti-humanist teaching, but they were not the first to maintain it. ...

This extreme 'Nominalism', which Bremond saw and condemned as a precursor of anti-humanism, is not the only thing that ought to be said, even in a sketch such as this, about late medieval thought and the climate of opinion it was breeding. Although William of Ockham was probably the thinker who was most destructive of 'intellectualism' as it has been explained, and one who drove a wedge between philosophy and theology, the scene is far more complex than this apparently simple opposition between the *Via Antiqua* and the *Via Moderna* would seem to imply.

There was, for instance, Gabriel Biel, a German theologian who entered the University of Heidelberg in 1432 and spent time also in the Universities of Erfurt, Cologne and Tübingen. Continental universities by this time tended to be divided between those which taught the *Via Antiqua*, like Cologne, and those which upheld the *Via Moderna*, like Erfurt. To Biel it seemed a good thing that the older, canonized doctors like Aquinas could be openly contradicted in the schools, and this view he adopted without ridiculing them. Biel himself was a qualified Nominalist. He thought that only God was absolutely necessary, but that his activity was unpredictable, not arbitrary. The human reason was capable of a few insights about God: that he exists and is wise; that knowledge about him was not self-evident but could be acquired through experience; that faith was necessary but was not *contrary* to natural reason; and that God had created a natural order in which men were capable of acting well whether they were believers or not. For him, revealed doctrine was narrower than those who held to the *Via Antiqua* supposed, and tended to be restricted to factual information. The rest was a proper subject for speculation and natural reason. 'Use reason by which you can understand that God is, and call upon his help.' Cognition was for Biel, as it was for the medieval *Via Antiqua* and also the Council of Trent, the very root of all virtues, but in faith there was no inherent rational structure, and every single point of faith required a special act. The beginning of faith was assent to Scripture in its entirety. He therefore saw that theology was not a science in the true sense, but that there was no complete divorce between faith and reason because faith is awakened by 'semi-arguments'.

Above all, perhaps, Biel was a preacher and a pastoral theologian. He laid great store by preaching rather than by sterile debates, and associated himself with the Brethren of the Common Life, of whom more will be said in a moment. For him, education was all-important, for it made character. He was familiar with 'humanist' work, especially that of Pico della Mirandola, and when he retired from Tübingen he became provost of the new Brethren House at Einsiedel in Schönbuch where nobles, clergy and burgesses dwelt together according to the ideals of the Brethren's piety. In this way he forms a powerful link between the apparently contradictory tendencies of the late Middle Ages: the old way, the new way, secular humanism and the simple, affective faith of the *devotio moderna*. In the practical order faith came from preaching; *'fides ex auditu'*, and this was the beginning of salvation.

We may select another figure, not because he was the founder of a philosophical school — indeed, he stands very much on his own — but because he was one of the outstanding men of his age and in some ways he too looks back to medievalism and forward to the scientific mentality of the early modern period. This is Nicholas of Cusa, a reforming bishop in Germany, and ultimately a cardinal, who died in 1464. He cannot be called a heretic or a rebel. But he was certainly obsessed with the infinity, transcendence and incomprehensibility of the divine, and was hardly at home in the world of legalistic

Nicholas of Cusa (d. 1464), with St Peter and an angel. Funerary monument, *c.* 1500. 'Our knowledge of creatures is only approximate, for their truth is hidden in God.'

morality and mechanical piety. Cusa delighted in scientific studies, and he had above all a mathematical mind, seeing in the science of numbers and figures the most perfect mode of humanly knowing what was true. He felt the chasm that exists between physical objects on the one hand, with all their imperfections and crudities, and the pure, immaterial notions of mathematics which are perfectly true, without the limitations and approximations that physical matter imposes. Here is a quotation from one of his works:

> Everyone knows that in mathematics truth can be more surely reached than in the other liberal arts.... The geometrician does not care for lines and figures as they are in themselves, although they are not found outside [concrete] substances. He beholds with the eye of sense figures of the sensible world, in order that with the eye of the mind he may be able to behold the figures of the mind. Nor does the mind see the mental figures any the less truly than does the eye the sensible figures, but rather *all the more truly*, inasmuch as the mind beholds the figures in themselves, freed from material otherness [*alteritas*]. Ordinary physical perception cannot reach them without that otherness, for the figure acquires otherness from its union with material substance, which varies and varies. On account of this there is one triangle on this pavement and another on the wall, and [the figure] always falls short of a higher degree of truth and precision. But mental perception in the abstract will see the figures free from all variable otherness, since the mind discovers itself when the otherness of the senses is not there to perceive it. . . .

It will be noticed that Cusa is here saying more or less the same thing that our own mathematics teachers were trying to convey when they told us in the lower forms at school that for constructional geometry we must bring very sharp and hard pencils and draw very lightly and carefully; and yet that however neat and light we were, we still could do no more than produce a gross approximation to a circle or a triangle. Cusa, of course, was going further, and was reaffirming the power of the intellect to grasp truths, and was expressing his dissatisfaction with the limitations and imperfections of mere sense experience. This was a whole world away from Ockham and his followers, for whom a real triangle could only be a term, non-existent in reality, and serving only as a notion to signify the observed characteristics of triangularity in the physical world. But at the same time, Cusa was much removed from the scholastics of the *Via Antiqua*, and the Thomists, who thought to apprehend God with the intellect. For Cusa intellectual truths were mathematical ones and did not add to our knowledge of God or ultimate reality. In fact, Cusa held that the intellectual approach to God could only be by way of negation. Since he is infinite, nothing definite could be said of him ('predicated of him') by human beings, since all definite descriptions or attributions of qualities necessarily likened him to finite things and brought him into relation with them, which was hopelessly wrong. We cannot, for instance, call God great or small. Any quality we can think of (except that of infinitude) implies an absence of the opposite quality, and God cannot be limited by the absence of any quality. He is indeed the harmonization of all opposites. So we have to admit that he surpasses our knowledge and is inaccessible to our own discursive reasoning. We cannot penetrate his nature. We are ignorant of him, and know only *that* he is. This is not the ignorance of indifference, or inertia, but of psychological limitation. Hence, our ignorance is 'learned' or instructed ignorance (*docta ignorantia*), and this phrase of his, 'learned ignorance', is often used to sum up Cusa's attitude. It is, in its way, a kind of agnosticism, not of the modern sort, but of a metaphysical variety, because it accepted God's existence out of a mode of mathematical necessity but said that no more could be philosophically known. There are senses in which Aquinas was a rationalist and Cusa an agnostic.

To put Cusa's ideas in a more general setting, he said that there were three levels of human knowledge:

Sense perception, which can affirm only; that is, our senses tell us positive things; by definition, anything we perceive by eye or nose or touch is *there*.

Secondly, there is *ratio*, which is discursive reason, whose instrument is language; *ratio* can both affirm and deny — this is so, that is not so; this is what we mean in ordinary speech by human reason.

And lastly, there is *intellectus*, which apprehends God, but is capable of denying only; after the first, obscure apprehension *that* he is, there is nothing else possible but to deny that he is this, that or the other. *What* he is cannot be stated, as he is above language.

It will be apparent that Nicholas of Cusa as a devout believer was thrown back upon a sort of mystical intuition, and in this he is entirely in line with the later medieval mystics who played such a large part in the life of the Church at that epoch. For all of them, as for mystics generally, God dwelt in a Cloud of Unknowing. And in a sublime way Cusa mirrors the attitude of many devout persons in Europe, whether they lived in the cloister, like the Carthusians, or in communities of a new sort, like the Brethren of the Common Life in the Low Countries, or whether they were the layfolk who were even then reading and living by works like *The Imitation of Christ* by Thomas à Kempis.

Clearly, it is impossible to do justice to the many-sided richness of late medieval theology and philosophy in an essay of this nature. Even primary research on it has not progressed far. There were also less typical characters, like Reginald Pecock, Bishop of Chichester, who died under condemnation about 1460. His actual condemnation was for political rather than theological reasons, but he was certainly not in general tune with the times, for he may be described as an extreme 'intellectualist' of a new sort, who believed that the 'truths of faith' could be demonstrated by the human reason, and in his primary, self-imposed task of confuting the Lollards, laid great stress upon what he called the 'doom of reason', which was to say, the decisions of the human reason, arrived at rationally. He wrote in English, and invented a number of new words which made him very difficult to understand. He also believed, like so many of his contemporaries, in the value of preaching, and held that the English bishops, 'dumb dogs who could not bark', had failed in their pastoral efforts. But again, this learned man, seemingly remote from the aspirations and anxieties of the vulgar populace, supplies links with the common man's simpler religion of faith and works. Apart from him, England has, so far as we know, little to offer in the way of intellectual leadership in the late Middle Ages.

At the end we come back to late medieval piety because it demonstrates in a more practical and everyday manner the 'flight from intellect'. A leading movement of this piety is sometimes known as the *Devotio Moderna*, and it forms an interesting parallel with the philosophical *Via Moderna*, about which something has now been written. The *Devotio Moderna* was a practical mysticism, or, as it is sometimes described, a form of affective piety that appealed to the heart and not to the head. It began in the Netherlands, and one of its founders was Gerard de Groot, who was born in 1340, just towards the end of Ockham's life. Gerard's followers founded the Communities of the Common Life, at Deventer and Windesheim and elsewhere, where they followed a rule, lived simply, and copied devotional manuscripts which had a wide use and popularity. Their influence was felt also in Germany and France. They wrote in short sentences and were fond of maxims. They were contemptuous of human knowledge and suspicious of the legalistic life of ecclesiastical institutions, benefices, universities and the rest. The *Imitation of Christ*, so popular in more modern times, expresses this view clearly:

How does it profit you to reason profoundly about the Trinity if you lack humility and thus make yourself displeasing to the Trinity? Truly, elevated discourses make you neither holy nor just, but rather is it by a virtuous life that you become dear to God. I much prefer to feel compunction than to know its definition. Check this lively appetite to know, for only great deception lies in it. . . .

Or again, from another book of the same *genre*, the *Enchiridion Vitae Spiritualis*:

Do not wish to know any other thing than Christ crucified. If you know him well your knowledge is enough, even if you are ignorant of all else. Study continually his life and passion. Consider *what* he suffered in order to suffer with him; *how* he suffered in order to imitate him; and *why* he suffered in order to respond to his charity by loving in your turn. Make to grow within you the continual desire to be able to conform in some measure to your Master, by bearing patiently all the trials which he may be pleased to impose upon you according to his good pleasure. . . .

Remote from English Lollardy though all this may at first sight seem, there was nevertheless a certain similarity of spirit between continental affective piety and English heterodoxy of the late Middle Ages. It would be a mistake to suppose that England at this time was neatly divided between the orthodox, who lived according to the apparatus of mechanical religion already described, and the Lollards, who were condemned and persecuted. There were men and women who were touched by the new spirit of the times who never became Lollards, or, if they did, recanted without changing their natures, or gave their simple hearts to an unintellectual pursuit of Christian excellence. To add to the confusion, Wyclif, so often (mistakenly) thought of as the founder of the Lollard sect, was himself an extreme philosophical Realist and no Nominalist. But like his more naïve successors he turned against the apparatus of mediated religion, rejecting in the end the priestly claims of extreme sacramentalism and the reservation to clergy alone of the interpretation of the scriptures. Lollards, and those near to them, were 'Bible men', reading the scriptures (or favourite parts of them) in English and committing them to memory, insisting upon the virtues as against theology and the schools, storming against the parsons. Their zeal affected many and 'respectable' men. Leading burgesses became interested. Hereford, one of Wyclif's supporters, preached before the Mayor of Leicester in 1382, saying especially that God had never ordered the Mass to be celebrated and that it would be better to have fewer Masses. Swinderby, an altogether wilder character — a woman-hater, if his enemies are to be believed — when excommunicated appealed to the king's justices in parliament and sent his conclusions to the knights of Parliament, addressing the royal Council as 'Dear, worshipful sirs in this world . . . as we see by many tokens that this world draws to an end . . . .'

177

There are undercurrents of social protest mingled with this millenarianism. In truth the world was not drawing to an end, but a new one was beginning.

The late medieval epoch is not famous among the general public for its religious zeal or the soundness of its ecclesiastical life. Unfortunately or fortunately, much of what was best in the religious life and thought of the age was in tune with a pious yet obscurantist attitude. It was an attitude met in many places and many ways: amongst ecclesiastics, theologians, preachers and layfolk, sensible or half-crazed. But I think we have to admit that the philosophical attitudes and the devotional attitudes which have been fleetingly encountered in this chapter on 'the flight from intellect' go in some ways together and give to the age its own special brand of weakness and strength, and perhaps also help to explain the confusion in which many men found themselves when they suddenly became confronted in the 1530s with certain dire and practical problems.

Sources and Further Reading

This is not, and could not be, a full bibliography. The chapters of this book have been put together partly from original evidence, both printed and manuscript, and partly from other people's researches. It was decided to use footnotes mainly to identify original sources, so that the pages of the text did not become littered in a way that would be irritating to non-specialists. It is hoped that these notes, and the List of Abbreviations, will serve to identify most of the original material. For the rest, I must ask scholars and writers whose work I have used to forgive me for not acknowledging it wherever it occurs. I have tried to make amends in this note.

This section therefore has a double function. It is meant in the first place to show what books and articles happen especially to have helped and interested me in the composition of the book, so that readers who are similarly interested may be passed on to them. In the second place it is intended to acknowledge my debts with as much propriety as possible. If there are serious omissions they are accidental, and pardon is asked of anyone who feels himself cheated of due recognition. Some works, of course, have been useful for more than one chapter even though they are generally cited under one chapter-heading only. It goes without saying that any historian who writes a general book has benefited from a great deal of reading which he does not directly use or cite.

Chapter 1

Writers on late medieval England whose viewpoint I often do not share but whose work is to be recommended are William Stubbs, *The Constitutional History of England* (many editions), vol. III; W. Denton, *England in the fifteenth century* (1888); David Knowles, *The Religious Orders in England*, vol. II: *The End of the Middle Ages* (1955), and vol. III: *The Tudor Age* (1959). The view that the late Middle Ages was a time of waning and decay, whatever else of brilliance was happening in courtly, artistic or literary circles, is expressed in two well-known classics: Jacob Burckhardt, *The Civilization of the Renaissance* (first published in 1860, and in many editions since), and J. Huizinga, *The Waning of the Middle Ages* (transl. F. Hopman, Penguin Books, 1955).

In the second rank are numerous books on later medieval England which are, in various senses, competitors with this one: H. S. Bennett, *The Pastons and their England* (2nd ed., 1932), which is a descriptive book by a predominantly literary historian; Percival Hunt, *Fifteenth-century England* (Pittsburgh and London, 1962), a slight sketch; and J. R. Lander, *The Wars of the Roses* (1965). Professor Lander, whose work I greatly admire, has also written a number of scholarly articles, and has told me he is preparing a more general short book on this period, though his interests are perhaps more 'aristocratic' than mine.

Chapter 2

On the questions of nationhood and the 'Identity of England' the following are useful: G. Warner's edition of *The Libelle of Englyshe Polycye* (Oxford, 1926); V. H. Galbraith, 'Nationality and Language in Medieval England', *Transactions of the Royal Historical Society*, 4th series, XXIII (1941), pp. 113–29; Barnaby C. Keeney, 'Military Service and the Development of Nationalism in England, 1272–1327', *Speculum*, XXII (1947), pp. 534–49; L. R. Loomis, 'Nationality at the Council of Constance', *American Historical Review*, XLIV (1939), pp. 508–27; R. Flenley, 'London and Foreign Merchants in the Reign of Henry VI', *English Historical Review*, XXV (1910), pp. 644–55; M. M. Postan, 'The Economic and Political Relations of England and the Hansa from 1400 to 1475', in *Studies in English Trade in the Fifteenth Century* (ed. Eileen Power and M. M. Postan, 1933, reprinted 1951), pp. 91–153.

The language question is treated by H. S. Bennett, 'The Author and His Public in the Fourteenth and Fifteenth Centuries', *Essays and Studies*, XXIII (1937), pp. 7–24; G. L. Brook, *English Dialects* (1963), especially Chapter 3; and R. E. Zachrisson, 'Notes on the Essex Dialect and the Origin of London Vulgar Speech', in *Englische Studien*, Bd. 59 (1925), pp. 346–60.

Froissart's Chronicle has recently been excerpted and translated in a popular edition by Geoffrey Brereton, *Froissart's Chronicles* (Penguin Classics, 1968). War and Chivalry receive more realistic treatment from Denys Hay, 'The Divisions of the Spoils of War in Fourteenth-Century England', *T.R.H.S.*, 5th series, vol. IV, pp. 91–109; and Maurice Keen, *The Laws of War in the Late Middle Ages* (1965). Both the logistics and the sufferings of warfare are described by H. J. Hewitt in *The Organization of War under Edward III* (1966). War-torn France may be better understood through Robert Boutruche, *La Crise d'une Société: Seigneurs et paysans du Bordelais pendant la Guerre de Cent Ans* (1963), and Guy Fourquin, *Les Campagnes de la Région parisienne à la fin du Moyen Age* (1964). On travel, inside and outside England, see *The Itinerary of William Worcester*, ed. J. Nasmith (Cambridge, 1788); *The Stacions of Rome and the Pilgrims' Sea Voyage*, ed. F. J. Furnivall (*Early English Text Society*, 1867); and David Quinn, 'Edward IV and Exploration', *The Mariners' Mirror*, vol. XXI (1935), pp. 275–85, though Professor Quinn has subsequently realized that *explorator* meant spy and not explorer.

Chapter 3

It is even more difficult to be concise and selective in recommending further reading on the economy of this age. The best beginning is perhaps J. E. Thorold Rogers, *A History of Agriculture and Prices*, especially vol. I (1866) and vol. II (1882), and his readable summary called *Six Centuries of Work and Wages* (1908), especially Chapter 3. Everything written by Professor M. M. Postan is worth reading, and one may single out 'Revisions in Economic History: the fifteenth century', in *Economic History Review*, IX (1938–9), pp. 160–7; 'Some Evidence of the Declining Population in the Later Middle Ages', *Ec.H.R.*, 2nd series, vol. II (1950), pp. 221–46, and his argument against the late K. B. McFarlane, that England did not profit by the war, in 'The Costs of the Hundred Years' War', *Past and Present*, No. 27 (1964), pp. 34–53. Likewise, all Professor E. M. Carus-Wilson's contributions are invaluable. Many of her studies are brought together in *Medieval Merchant Venturers* (1954), and she has reprinted several papers of great value by different authors (which will not be itemized here) in *Essays in Economic History*, vol. I (1954, and subsequently reprinted), vol. II (1962). Heady stimulus is to be derived from A. R. Bridbury's essay, *Economic Growth: England in the Later Middle Ages* (1962), though he has little to say about the countryside. On this subject Professor R. H. Hilton is worth reading with respect, for example, in *A Medieval Society: the Western Midlands at the End of the Thirteenth Century* (1966). He promises a sequel on the later Middle Ages.

More technical economic argument about western Europe's condition is to be found in E. Perroy, 'A l'origine d'une économie contractée: les crises du XIVᵉ siècle', *Annales* (1949), pp. 167–82, and H. A. Miskimin, 'Monetary Movements and Market Structure — Forces for Contraction in Fourteenth and Fifteenth-Century England', *Journal of Economic History*, vol. XXIV (1964), pp. 470–90. For France, the works of Boutruche and Fourquin, already cited under Chapter 2, should be noted. On Germany there is W. Abel, *Geschichte der deutschen Landwirtschaft* (Stuttgart, 1962), especially Chapter 3; also the same author's *Die Wüstungen des ausgehenden Mittelalters* (2nd ed., Stuttgart, 1955); and 'Wüstungen und Preisfall im Spätmittelalterlichen Europa', *Jahrbücher für Nationalökonomie und Statistik*, Bd. 165 (1953), pp. 380–427.

A beginning on the 'lost village' problem in England may be made with the classic *Lost Villages of England* by Professor Maurice Beresford (1954), and to this may be added, as one example, K. Allinson, *The Deserted Villages of Northamptonshire* (Leicester University Press, 1966).

No reading list on population studies, so basic to our theme, would be complete without reference to J. Cox Russell, *British Medieval Population* (Albuquerque, New Mexico, 1948), though his arguments are sometimes obscure. Studies on the effects of the plague have progressed from J. Saltmarsh, 'Plague and Economic Decline in England in the Later Middle Ages', *Cambridge Historical Journal*, vol. VII (1941–3), pp. 23–41, to J. M. W. Bean, 'Plague, Population and Economic Decline in the Later Middle Ages', *Ec.H.R.*, 2nd series, vol. XV (1963), pp. 423–7, with a wider view by Elisabeth Carpentier, 'Autour de la peste noire: famines et épidémies dans l'histoire du XIVᵉ siècle', *Annales* (1962).

An article of which unashamedly large use has been made here is R. S. Schofield, 'The Geographical Distribution of Wealth in England, 1334–1649', *Ec.H.R*, 2nd series, vol. XVIII (1965), pp. 483–510.

The literature on towns is enormous and of uneven quality. The following may be singled out: T. F. Tout, 'The Beginnings of a Modern Capital: London and Westminster in the Fourteenth Century', *Collected Papers*, III (1934), pp. 249–75; Sylvia Thrupp, *The Merchant Class of Medieval London* (Chicago, 1948); W. G. Hoskins, 'English Provincial Towns in the Early Sixteenth Century', *T.R.H.S.*, 5th series, vol. VI (1956), pp. 1–19, reprinted in the same author's *Provincial England* (1963) as Chapter 4; J. N. Bartlett, 'The Expansion and Decline of York in the Later Middle Ages', *Ec.H.R.*, 2nd series, vol. XII (1959–60), pp. 17–33; E. L. Sabine, 'Butchering in Medieval London', *Speculum*, vol. VIII (1933), pp. 335–53. Information on east coast shipping comes from G. V. Scammel, 'English Merchant Shipping at the End of the Middle Ages: Some East Coast Evidence', *Ec.H.R.*, 2nd series, vol. XIII (1961), pp. 327–41. The Durham Iron-master was found as long ago as 1899 by G. Lapsley, *E.H.R.*, XIV (1899), pp. 509–29.

A brilliant and rapid essay on the urban middle classes, especially in Germany, is Fritz Rörig's *The Medieval Town* (English transl., 1967). Maurice Beresford's *New Towns of the Middle Ages* (1967) is also valuable.

The section on the countryside is based more fully on my own researches: 'A rentier economy in the later Middle Ages: the Archbishopric of Canterbury', in *Ec.H.R.*, 2nd series, vol. XVI (1964), pp. 427–38; 'Who were farming the English demesnes at the end of the Middle Ages?', *Ec.H.R.*, 2nd series, vol. XVII (1965), pp. 443–55; and *The Lordship of Canterbury: an Essay on Medieval Society* (1966); but a debt to Professor R. H. Hilton's work will also be obvious, and there is some interesting material in T. Jones-Pierce, 'Some Tendencies in the Agricultural History of Caernarvonshire during the Later Middle Ages', *Transactions of the Caernarvonshire Historical Society*, vol. I(1939), pp. 18—36; and *The Book of William Morton, almoner of Peterborough Monastery, 1448—1467* (transcribed and annotated by W. T. Mellows, edited by P. I. King, with introductions by C. N. L. Brooke and M. M. Postan), Northamptonshire Record Society, vol. XVI (1954).

Chapter 4

My interest in this topic was first aroused by Sir George Sitwell's article 'The English Gentleman' in *The Ancestor*, vol. I (1902), pp. 58—103; the same author produced more information in *The Hurts of Holdsworth* (1930). His work seemed to provide an original synthesis until the discovery of Karl D. Bülbring's introduction to Daniel Defoe's *Compleat Gentleman* (London, 1890), pp. xxxii–lxxxiv, suggested that Sitwell's paper itself had an ancestor. In any case, Sitwell went too far in supposing that the "gentry" suddenly sprang into existence in the fifteenth century; nor is it true that they were simply younger sons of aristocratic and knightly families, let alone merely those affected by stock-and-land leasing. There is a lot of discursive information in Professor Sylvia Thrupp's book, already cited under Chapter 3, and she also deals with class feelings in 'The Problem of Conservatism in Fifteenth-Century England', *Speculum*, vol. 18 (1943), pp. 363—8. The question of armorial bearings, amongst others, is treated by A. R. (now Sir Anthony) Wagner in *Heralds and Heraldry in the Middle Ages* (Oxford, 1956). A classic article which set off a controversy is R. H. Tawney, 'The Rise of the Gentry', in *Ec.H.R.*, vol. XI (1941), pp. 1—38. This paper and the controversy mainly concern the sixteenth and seventeenth centuries, and those interested had better look in the back files of *Past and Present*, but Tawney is mentioned here as an original stimulant and a *fons et origo*. The controversy is summarized in Lawrence Stone's *Social change and revolution in England, 1540—1640* (1965).

Continental work of relevance here is obtainable in Jacques Heers, *L'Occident au XIVe et XVe siècles: aspects économiques et sociaux* (Paris, 1963); E. Perroy, 'Social Mobility among the French Noblesse in the Later Middle Ages', *Past and Present*, No. 21 (April, 1962), pp. 25—38; Charles de Ribbe, *La Société provençale à la fin du moyen âge, d'après des documents inédits* (Paris, 1898); and Georges Duby, *L'Economie rurale et la vie des campagnes dans l'Occident médiéval*, t. 2 (Paris, 1962). Rörig's book, referred to under Chapter 3, is useful for its glimpse of class-feelings in Germany.

Returning to England, more specialized aspects are treated by K. L. Wood-Legh, 'Sheriffs, Lawyers and Belted Knights in the Parliaments of Edward III', *E.H.R.*, XLVI (1931), pp. 372—88; E. W. Ives, 'Promotion in the Legal Profession of Yorkist and Early Tudor England', *Law Quarterly Review*, vol. 75 (1959), pp. 348—63; E. F. Jacob, *The Register of Archbishop Chichele, 1414—1443*, vol. II (Oxford, 1938), introduction. Besides this, there are numerous printed collections of wills which, used with care, are a first-rate source.

Such are *Lincoln Wills*, ed. C. W. Foster, vol. I: *1271–1526* (1914), Lincoln Record Society V; *Wills and Inventories from the registers of the Commissary of Bury St. Edmunds and the archdeaconry of Sudbury*, ed. Samuel Tymms, Camden Society, o.s. XLIX (1850); *English Wills, 1498–1526*, ed. A. F. Cirket, Bedfordshire Historical Records Society Publications, vol. XXXVII (1957); F. J. Furnivall, *The Fifty Earliest English Wills*, *E.E.T.S.*, old series, vol. 78 (1882); *Some Oxfordshire Wills proved in the Prerogative Court of Canterbury, 1393–1510*, Oxfordshire Record Society (1958).

A useful collection of sumptuary legislation, 1363–1533, was made in an article in *Complaint and Reform in England*, arranged by W. H. Dunham and S. Pargellis (Oxford, 1938), pp. 31–50.

The fifteenth-century political and social scene has been analysed directly from record sources by R. L. Storey, *The End of the House of Lancaster* (1966). Other key works on fifteenth-century English politics which illuminate the noble class are K. B. McFarlane, 'Bastard Feudalism', *B.I.H.R.*, vol. XX (1943–5), and the same author's 'Wars of the Roses', in *Proceedings of the British Academy*, vol. 50 (1964); also W. H. Dunham, 'Lord Hastings' Indentured Retainers, 1461–83', *Transactions of the Connecticut Academy of Arts and Sciences* (New Haven, Conn.), vol. 39 (1955), pp. 1–175; this contains an excellent bibliography.

Later medieval books of etiquette or "nurture" attracted much attention from *The Early English Text Society*: for example, *The Babees Book*, ed. F. J. Furnivall, *E.E.T.S.*, old series, vol. 32 (1868). There is also *The Boke of Noblesse*, ed. J. G. Nichols, Roxburghe Club (1860), which was written in 1475 and extolled the old-fashioned view of chivalric knighthood at the expense of the countrified and peace-loving "knights" of the author's own day.

For the literary angle, see Sir Edmund K. Chambers, *English Literature at the Close of the Middle Ages* (Oxford History of English Literature, reprinted 1947 with corrections), especially the chapter on Malory.

On the development of the English language and the question of provincial and class speech there is the text-book by A. C. Baugh, *History of the English Language* (New York, many editions), and the article by Zachrisson, already cited under Chapter 2. Here I should like to thank my colleague, Dr G. C. Britten, for the characteristically painstaking help he has given me.

Some *obiter dicta* on the change in the treatment of women during the fourteenth century occur in C. D. Ross's 'Forfeiture for Treason in the Reign of Richard II', *E.H.R.*, vol. LXXI (1956), pp. 560–75.

For the classes below the gentry, see Mildred Campbell, *The English Yeoman under Elizabeth and the Early Stuarts* (Yale, 1945), Appendix I: 'Early Usage of the Word Yeoman'; W. G. Hoskins, *The Midland Peasant* (1957), and several articles reprinted in *Essays in Economic History*, vol. II (1962). Many ideas were started by E. J. Hobsbawm's *Primitive Rebels* (Manchester, 1959).

Chapter 5

Quite a lot has been written on the theoretical or legal aspects of marriage in the Middle Ages. It would be no bad thing to begin by referring to an anthropological introduction which does not deal with Christendom but reminds us that the world is wider than that: Robin Fox, *Kinship and Marriage* (Penguin Books, 1967). On the Roman canon law and the Catholic Church's view, see Derrick Sherwin Bailey, *The Man-Woman Relationship in Christian Thought* (1959); the introduction by Canon Eric Kemp to *Papal Decretals relating to the Diocese of Lincoln in the Twelfth Century*, ed. Walther Holtzmann, Lincoln Record Society, vol. 47 (1954), pp. xxvi–xxviii; A. Esmein, *Le Mariage en droit canonique*, 2 vols (2nd ed. by R. Génestal and J. Dauvillier, Paris, 1929 and 1935); J. Dauvillier, *Le Mariage dans le droit classique de l'église* (Paris, 1933). An interesting exercise is to read consecutively the article 'Marriage' in the *Encyclopaedia Britannica* (Malinowski) and the article '*Mariage*' in the *Dictionnaire de Théologie catholique* (G. Le Bras).

On the English Common Law of Marriage, see F. Pollock and F. W. Maitland, *A History of English Law to the time of Edward I* (2nd ed., 1911), vol. II, Chapter 7; T. F. T. Plucknett, *The Legislation of Edward I* (1949), Chapter 5: 'The Family'.

There is much less written on the business side of medieval marriage, and even less on its personal aspects. But see H. S. Bennett's *The Pastons and their England*, already noted under Chapter 1; G. C. Homans, *English Villagers of the Thirteenth Century* (New York, 1941, since reprinted), Book 2; and the raw material in *Manners and Morals in Olden Time*, ed F. J. Furnivall, *E.E.T.S.*, old series, vol. 32 (1868), pp. 36–47.

Some continental comparisons have been made through Boutruche's book (see under Chapter 2, above); C. von Hoefler, *Die Aera der Bastarden am Schlusse des Mittelalters*, Boehm: Gesellschaft des Wissenschaft (Prague, 1891); H. Regnault, *La Condition juridique du bâtard au moyen âge* (Paris, 1923); R. Aubenas, 'L'Église et la Renaissance', which is t. 15 of A. Fliche et V. Martin, *Histoire de l'église*, pp. 327–8.

Chapter 6

Here again, the material has been drawn in small quantities from a fairly large variety of sources. On households and their organization, perhaps reference may be again permitted to the present writer's *Lordship of Canterbury* (1966), Chapter 6. There is also K. L. Wood-Legh, *A Small Household of the Fifteenth Century* (Manchester, 1956). On household accounting: C. D. Ross, 'Household Accounts of Elizabeth Berkeley Countess of Warwick, 1420–1', in *Transactions of the Bristol and Gloucestershire Archaeological Society*, vols. 70–1 (1951–2), pp. 81–105; M. E. James, 'Estate Accounts of the Earls of Northumberland, 1526–1637', *Surtees Society*, vol. 163 (1955), pp. xxiv-xxxiv.

A big debt is owing to Philippe Ariès, *Centuries of Childhood*, transl. Robert Baldick (1962).

Piers Plowman and François Villon, so often cited, are cheaply available in modern translations and paperback format: *Langland: Piers the Ploughman*, transl. by J. F. Goodrich (Penguin Books, 1959); *The Poems of François Villon*, French-English edition, ed. by Galway Kinnell (Signet Classics: The New American Library, 1965, with introduction and supplementary bibliography). The standard edition of *Piers the Plowman* is, of course, that by W. W. Skeat, 2 vols. (latest reprint with additional bibliography, 1961).

On inheritance, see two books already mentioned: F. Pollock and F. W. Maitland, *History of English Law*, especially vol. II, Chapter 6, and G. C. Homans, *English Villagers*, Book 2. Also F. Pollock, *The Land Laws* (1883), and A. W. B. Simpson, *An Introduction to the History of the Land Law* (1961).

There is a wealth of continental material, from which may be selected *Gedenkbuch des metzer Burgers Philippe von Vignelles aus den Jahren 1471 bis 1522...*, ed. Heinrich Michelaut (Stuttgart, 1852); M. Gonon, *La Vie familiale en Forez au XIVe siècle et son vocabulaire d'après les testaments* (Mâcon, 1960); Yvonne Bezard, *La Vie rurale dans la sud de la région parisienne de 1450 à 1560* (1929), criticized by Guy Fourquin in his book referred to above, under Chapter 2; R. Aubenas, 'La Famille dans l'ancienne Provence', in *Annales d'histoire économique et sociale*, no. 42 (Paris, 1936), pp. 523–41; Henri Auffroy, 'L'Évolution du testament en France des origines au XIIIe siècle' (Thèse pour le doctorat, Paris, 1899); Jean Engelmann, *Les Testaments coutumiers au XVe siècle* (1903); R. Aubenas, 'L'*Ordinatio pro anima* en Languedoc aux XVe et XVIe siècles', *Revue d'histoire de l'église de France*, t. XXIX (1943), pp. 257–62.

Chapter 7

This chapter can be given little supporting bibliography. Apart from the works of R. L. Storey and J. R. Lander, already noted under Chapter 4 and Chapter I, there is B. Wilkinson, *Constitutional History of England in the fifteenth century* (1964); B. L. Woodcock, *Medieval Ecclesiastical Courts in the diocese of Canterbury* (1952); W. H. Hale, *A Series of Precedents and Proceedings in criminal causes (1475–1640) extracted from the Act-Books of ecclesiastical courts in the diocese of London* (1847); E. W. Ives, 'The Reputation of the Common Lawyer in English society, 1450–1550', in *University of Birmingham Historical Journal*, vol. VII (1960), pp. 130–61, and the same author's 'The Common Lawyer in pre-Reformation England', *T.R.H.S.*, 5th series, XVIII (1968), pp. 145–73. I. Churchill's *Canterbury Administration* (1933) is also important. For the medical profession, there is *The Medical Practitioners in Medieval England: a Biographical Dictionary* (1965), by C. H. Talbot and E. A. Hammond, and C. H. Talbot's *Medicine in Medieval England* (1967).

Chapter 8

A learned and unsympathetic account is G. G. Coulton, *Five Centuries of Religion*, vol. IV (Cambridge, 1950). A systematic manual is the Fliche et Martin volume mentioned under Chapter 5, above. Another book of general interest is W. A. Pantin, *The English Church in the Fourteenth Century* (1955).

On the 'aristocratic' spiritually of the twelfth century, Etienne Gilson, *The Mystical Theology of St Bernard* (Engl. transl., Downes, 1940); Otto G. von Simson, 'The Gothic Cathedral: Design and Meaning', *Journal of the Society of Architectural Historians*, reprinted in *Change in Medieval Society*, ed. Sylvia Thrupp (London, 1965).

On the Dance of Death, A. Tenenti, *La Vie et La Mort à travers l'art du XVe siècle*, Cahiers des Annales (Paris, 1952); E. M. Manasse, 'The Dance Motiv in the Latin Dance of Death', *Medievalia et Humanistica* (Boulder, Colorado), vol. IV (1946), pp. 83—103. For examples of images in churches, *Thomas of Chillenden's Register*, ed. M. Mary de Sales (Brenda Duncombe) (London, unpublished M. A. thesis, 1963).

On English mysticism during this period, Helen Gardner, 'Walter Hilton and the Mystical Tradition in England', in *Essays and Studies*, XXII (1936), pp. 103—27.

For popular devotion, *John Myrc's Instructions for Parish Priests*, ed. Edward Peacock, *E.E.T.S.*, (1868); D. W. Robertson, 'The Cultural Tradition of *Handlyng Synne*', *Speculum*, XXII (1947), pp. 162—85; G. R. Owst, *Literature and the Pulpit in Medieval England* (2nd ed., Oxford, 1961); G. R. Owst, *The Destructio Viciorum of Alexander Carpenter: a fifteenth-century sequel to Literature and the Pulpit . . .* (1952). On the Mass, Francis Clark, *Eucharistic Sacrifice and the Reformation* (1960), and C. W. Dugmore, *The Mass and the English Reformers* (1958). On indulgences, W. E. Lunt, *Financial Relations of the Papacy with England, 1327–1534* (Medieval Academy of America, Publication No. 74, 1962), vol. II, Chapters 9—11. On chantries, K. L. Wood-Legh, *Perpetual Chantries in Britain* (1965); C. L. Kingsford, 'Our Lady of the Pew: the King's Oratory or Closet in the Palace of Westminster', *Archaeologia*, vol. 68 (1916—17), pp. 1—20.

On the significance of Piers Plowman, only a few of the great number of contributions are here suggested: R. W. Chambers, 'Piers Plowman, a Comparative Study', in *Man's Unconquerable Mind* (1939); Nevill K. Coghill, 'The character of Piers Plowman, considered from the B Text', in *Medium Aevum*, II (1933), pp. 108—35; T. P. Dunning, 'Langland and the Salvation of the Heathen', in *Medium Aevum*, XII (1943), pp. 45—54; R. W. Frank, 'The Pardon Scene in Piers Plowman', in *Speculum*, XXVI (1951), pp. 317—31.

Chapter 9

A general background which includes both Roscelin and Wyclif is provided by R. L. Poole, *Illustrations of Medieval Thought and Learning* (new ed., 1920). My account of Aquinas's 'intellectualism' has drawn heavily upon Pierre Rousselot, *The Intellectualism of St Thomas* (Engl. transl., 1935). Useful general books on medieval philosophy are E. Gilson, *History of Christian Philosophy in the Middle Ages*, part II (1955), and Frederick Coplestone, *History of Philosophy*, vol. II (1950), Chapters 31—41 (Aquinas); vol. III (1953), Chapters 3—9 (Ockham and the movement associated with him), Chapter 15 (Cusa). On Cusa, see also E. F. Jacob, *Essays in the Conciliar Epoch* (2nd ed., Manchester, 1952). The same collection contains work on the *'Devotio Moderna'*. On Gabriel Biel, see H. A. Oberman, *The Harvest of Medieval Theology: Gabriel Biel and Late Medieval Nominalism* (Harvard, 1963).

On Wyclif and Scripture, Michael Hurley, *'Scriptura Sola: Wyclif and his critics'*, in *Traditio*, XVI (1960), pp. 265—352, who controverts Dom De Vooght, *Les Sources de la doctrine chrétienne d'après les théologiens du XIVe siècle et du debut du XVe avec le texte intégral des XII premières questions de la Summa inédite du Gerard de Bologne* (Brussels, 1954).

The English bishop Reginald Pecock is treated by V. H. H. Green, *Bishop Reginald Pecock* (Cambridge, 1945), and E. F. Jacob, 'Reynold Pecock, Bishop of Chichester', *Proceedings of the British Academy*, vol. XXXVII (1951).

An old-fashioned but well-ordered manual on the history of spirituality which has been useful for late medieval pietism is P. Pourrat, *La Spiritualité chrétienne*, vol. II: *Le Moyen Âge* (ed. of 1951).

Index

(Page numbers in *italic type* indicate illustrations)